My First WORDS for SCHOOL

Part 1

T0103212

The word search below contains words from
For each picture, find and circle the correct
For the answers to this puzzle, see the answ

Earth in Space

☑

☐

Parts of a Flower

☐

☐

Weather

☐

☐

```
T F M O N T H Q Q S
E Q U A L J U D G E
M O H H U N D R E D
F J A L A S T E W S
I R R N W I S M H P
R A D D E B F A E V
S I O T E E P P N A
T N Q U K S S C H O
L Y F L O W E R O N
X M S V M O O N L W
```

Comparisons

☐ ☐

Counting

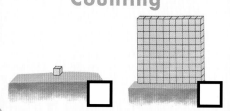

☐ ☐

Texture

☐ ☐

Places

☐ ☐

word Puzzle

ds from Part 2 of *My First Words for School*.
sing letters. The shared letters are already filled in.
swer key in *My First Words for School*.

KUM◯N

Down ⬇

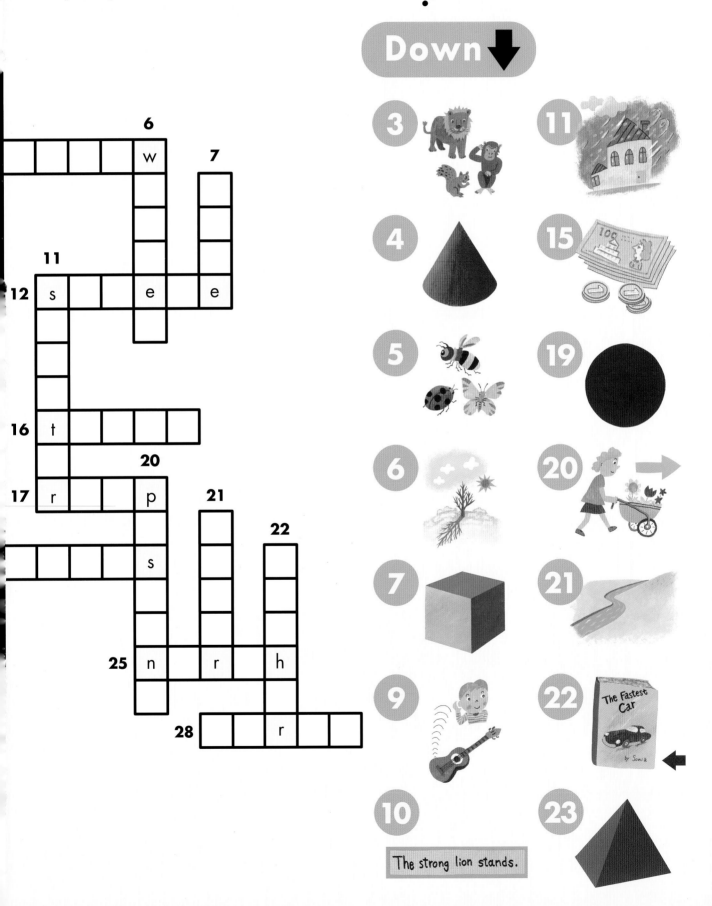

The strong lion stands.

My First WORDS for SCHOOL

Part 2

Crossw

The crossword puzzle below contains wor
Use the pictures as clues to fill in the miss
For the answers to this puzzle, see the an

Across ➡

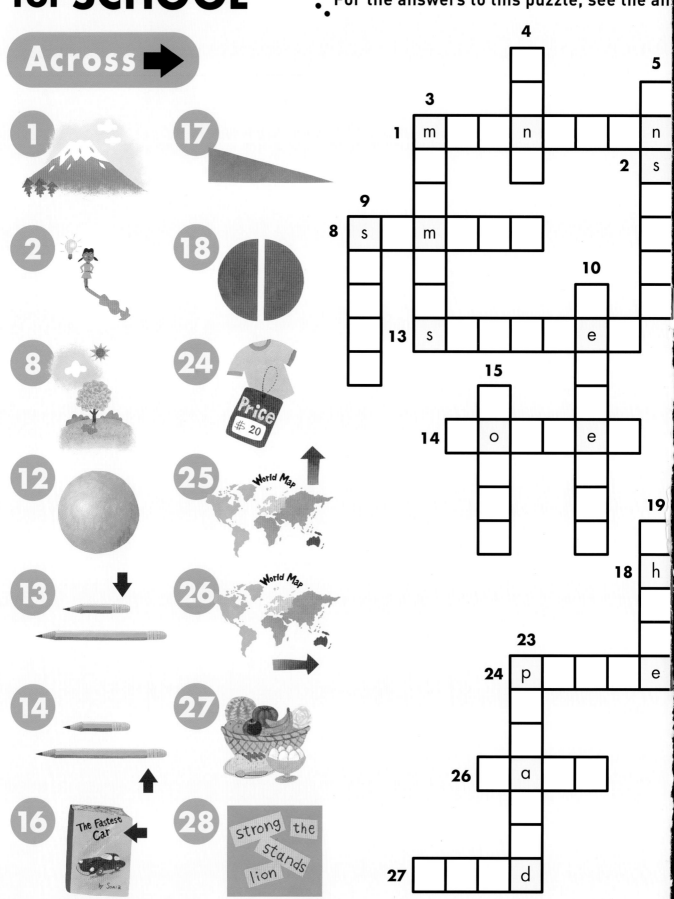

Search

Part 1 of *My First Words for School*.
word. The word *Earth* is shown as an example.
r key in *My First Words for School*.

S	P	B	S	I	D	E	S	V	X
O	E	L	E	G	E	N	D	G	N
F	A	A	W	R	E	P	L	A	Y
T	R	B	M	O	V	I	E	V	Y
U	T	T	C	O	R	N	E	R	S
D	H	S	T	O	R	E	J	T	B
R	T	I	S	T	J	M	S	L	G
O	L	B	W	D	L	O	V	E	O
H	W	H	E	R	E	R	Q	A	N
I	N	D	Y	V	U	E	V	F	E

The Calendar

Question Words

Position

Geometry

Jobs

Maps

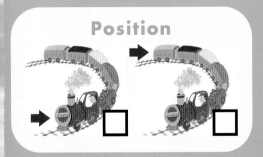

Story Time

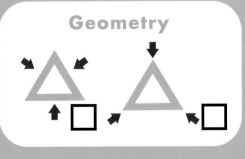

KUMON

My First WORDS for SCHOOL

Part 1

Table of Contents

Science Words
Earth in Space

■ Trace the letters while saying each word.

To parents/guardians:
In this section, your child will be introduced to reading and writing important words used in science. The pictures will help your child understand the meaning of each word. If your child asks why the word *Earth* is capitalized, explain that it is being used as a name—the name of a planet.

■ Trace the letters while saying each word.

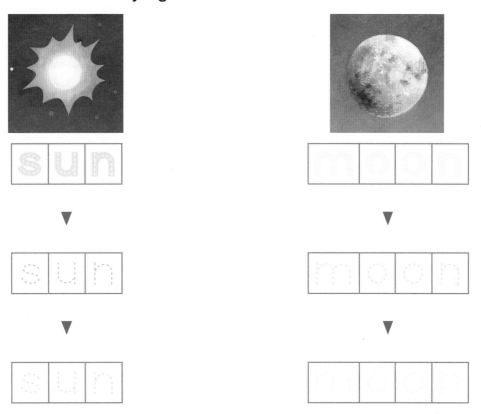

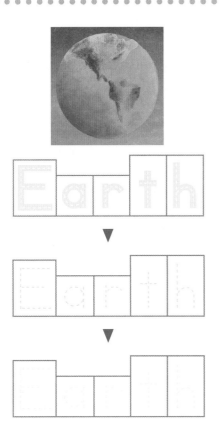

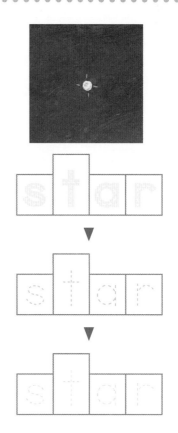

Science Words
Earth in Space

■ Trace each word. Then circle the correct picture.

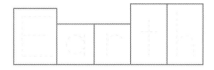

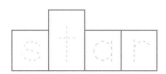

4

■ Trace and write the letters while saying each word.

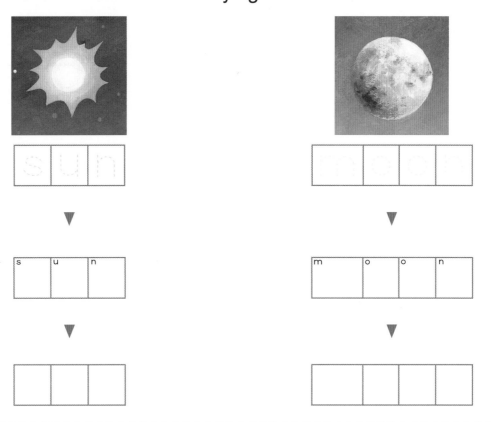

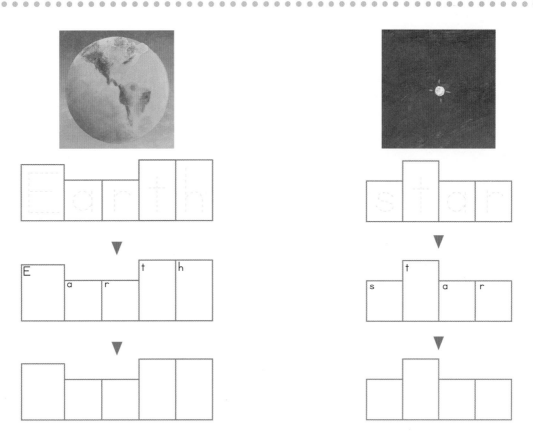

3 Science Words
Weather

Name

Date

■ Trace the letters while saying each word.

sunny

cloudy

rainy

windy

To parents/guardians:
Your child may need your help reading each word aloud at first. This book provides plenty of practice and repetition, so your child can eventually learn to read each word on their own.

■ Trace the letters while saying each word.

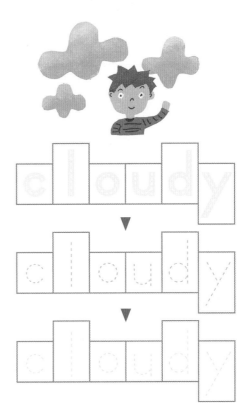

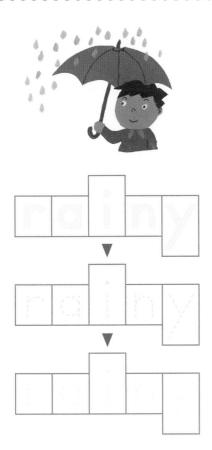

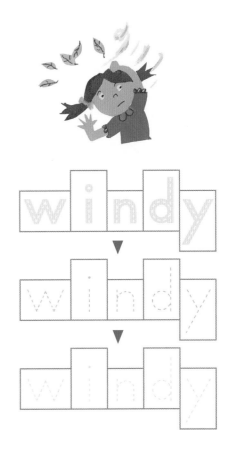

■ Trace each word. Then match each word with the correct picture.

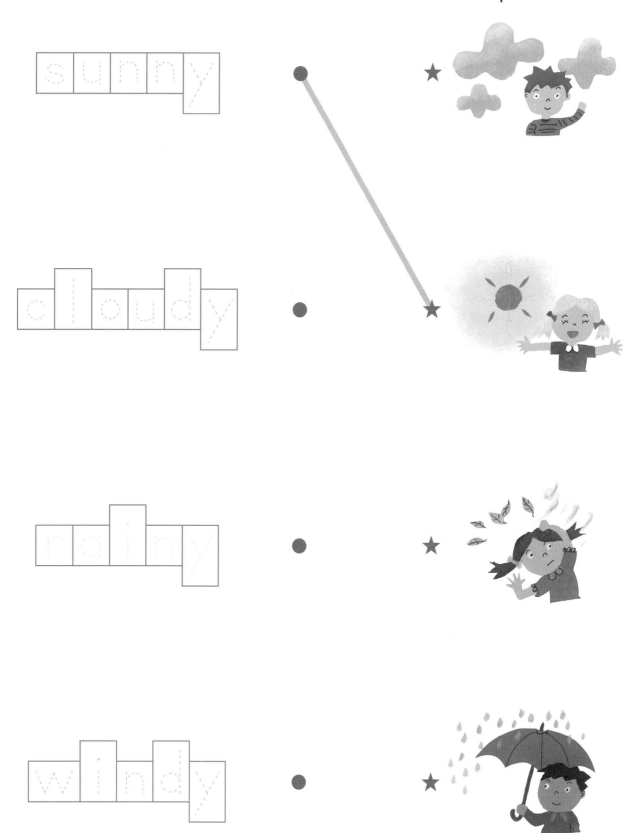

■ Trace and write the letters while saying each word.

Science Words

Texture

Name

Date

■ Trace the letters while saying each word.

soft

hard

bumpy

smooth

■ Trace the letters while saying each word.

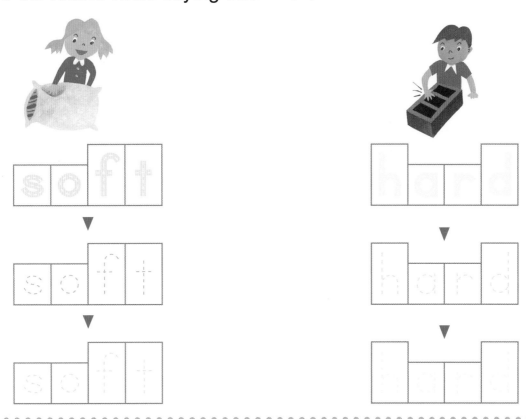

soft

▼

soft

▼

soft

hard

▼

hard

▼

hard

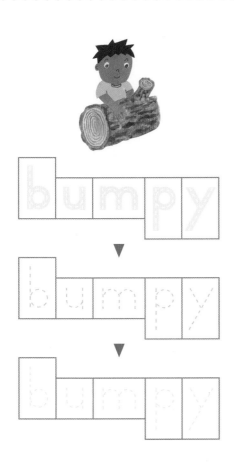

bumpy

▼

bumpy

▼

bumpy

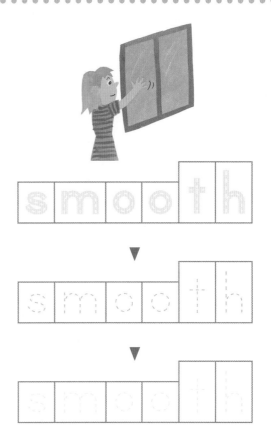

smooth

▼

smooth

▼

smooth

Science Words
Texture

Name

Date

■ Trace each word. Then match each word with the correct picture.

■ Trace and write the letters while saying each word.

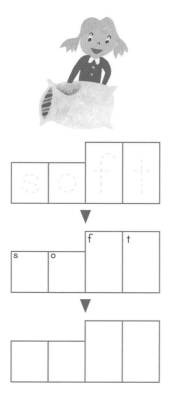

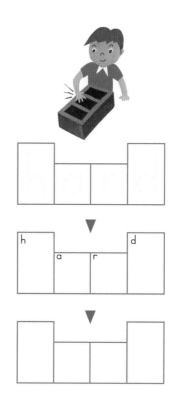

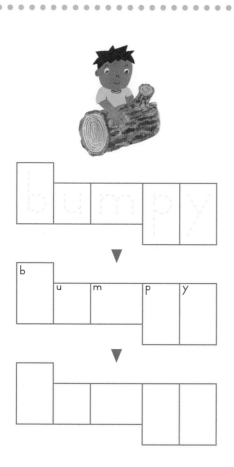

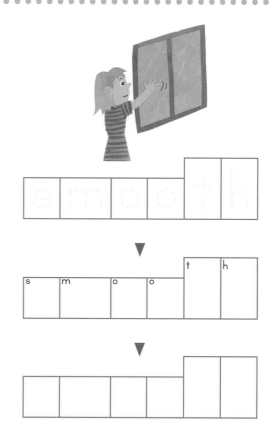

13

Science Words
Parts of a Flower

■ Trace the letters while saying each word.

■ Trace the letters while saying each word.

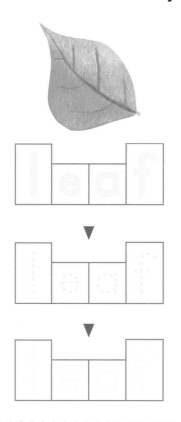

leaf

▼

leaf

▼

leaf

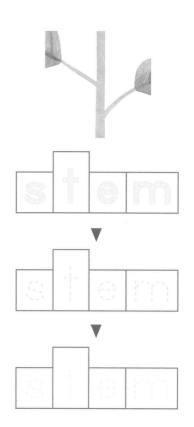

stem

▼

stem

▼

stem

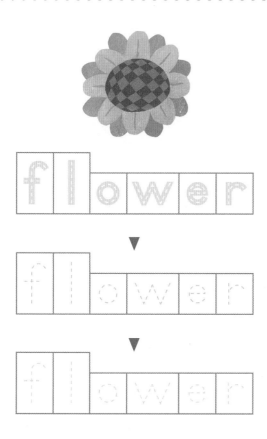

flower

▼

flower

▼

flower

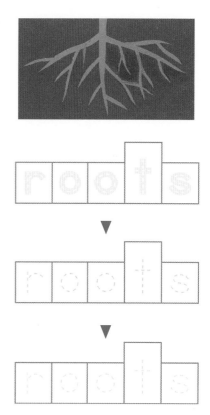

roots

▼

roots

▼

roots

Science Words

Parts of a Flower

■ Trace each word. Then circle the correct picture.

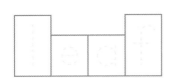

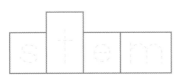

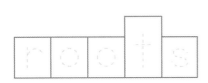

■ Trace and write the letters while saying each word.

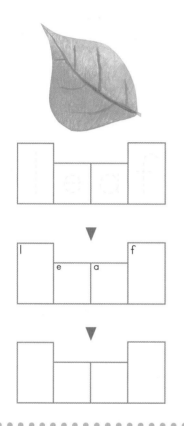

l e a f

l e a f

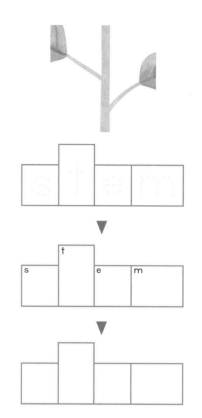

s t e m

s t e m

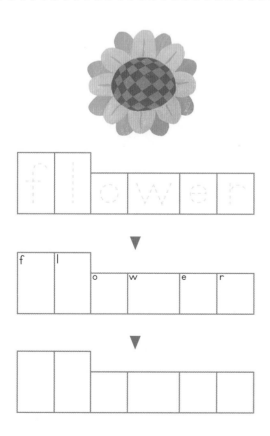

f l o w e r

f l o w e r

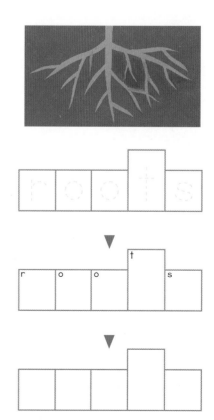

r o o t s

r o o t s

17

Science Words
Review

Name _____

Date _____

■ Write the letters while saying each word.

s	u	n

m	o	o	n

E	a	r	t	h

| | t | | |
| s | | a | r |

s	u	n	n	y

c	l	o	u	d	y

| | | i | | |
| r | a | | n | y |

| | i | | d | |
| w | | n | | y |

■ Write the letters while saying each word.

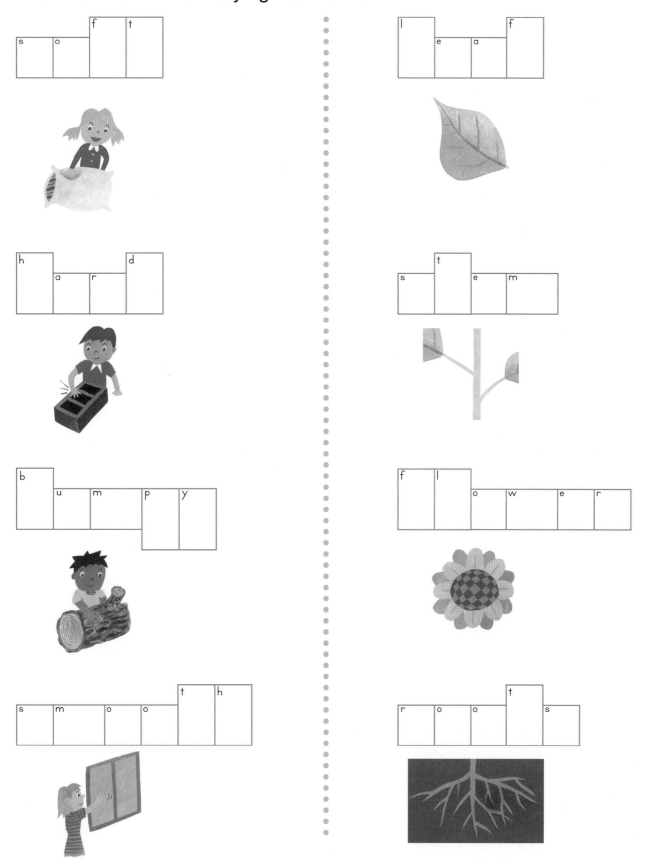

10 Math Words
Position

Name

Date

■ Trace the letters while saying each word.

To parents/guardians:
In this section, your child will be introduced to reading and
writing important words used in math. The pictures will help
your child understand the meaning of each word.

■ Trace the letters while saying each word.

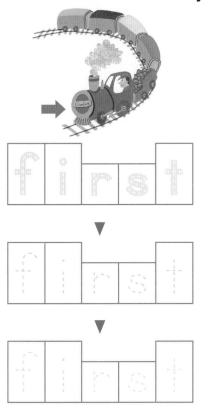

first

▼

first

▼

first

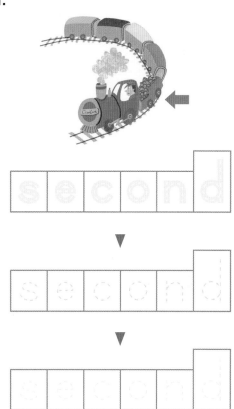

second

▼

second

▼

second

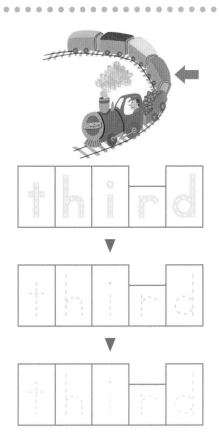

third

▼

third

▼

third

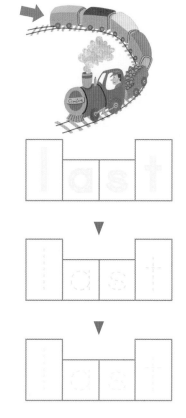

last

▼

last

▼

last

 **Math Words**
Position

■ Trace each word. Then match each word with the correct picture.

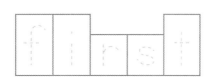   ●   ★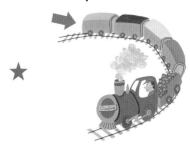

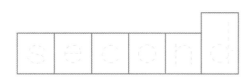   ●   ★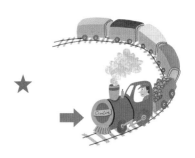

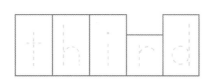   ●   ★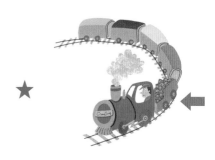

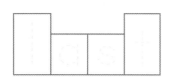   ●   ★

■ Trace and write the letters while saying each word.

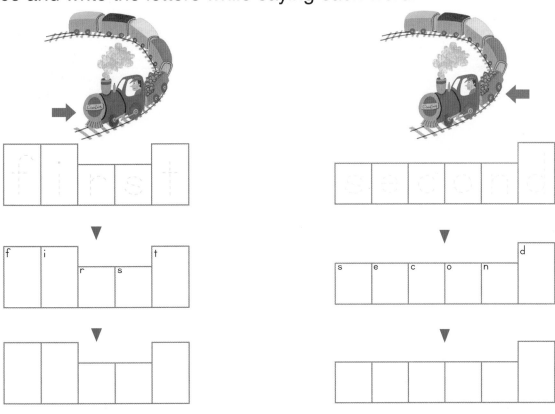

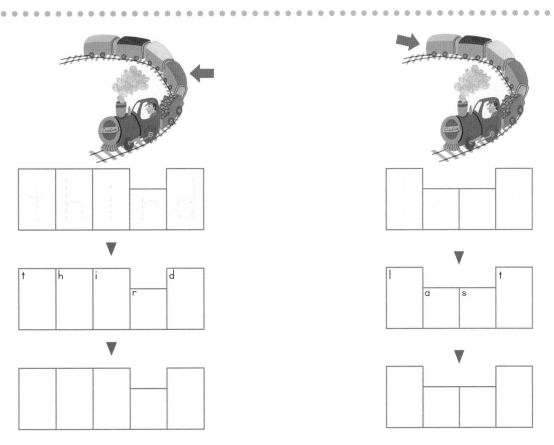

Math Words
Comparisons

Name

Date

■ Trace the letters while saying each word.

more

less

equal

24

■ Trace the letters while saying each word.

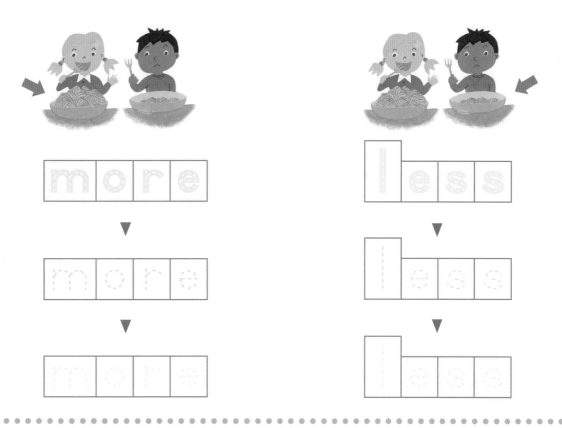

■ Trace each word. Then match each word with the correct picture.

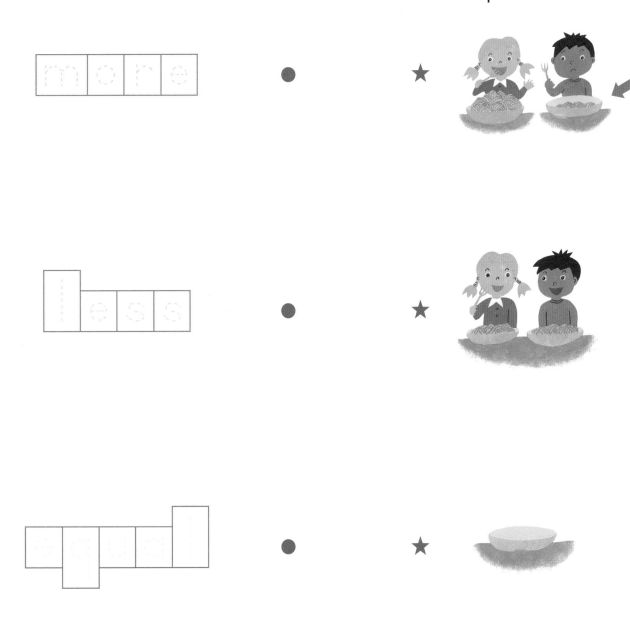

more   ●   ★

less   ●   ★

equal   ●   ★

none   ●   ★

■ Trace and write the letters while saying each word.

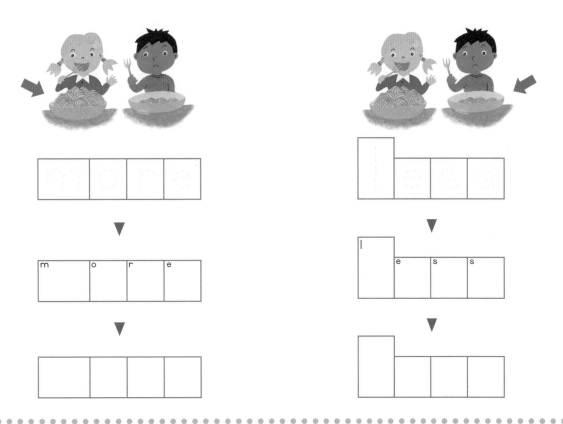

27

Math Words
Counting

Name

Date

■ Trace the letters while saying each word.

one

ten

hundred

zero

■ Trace the letters while saying each word.

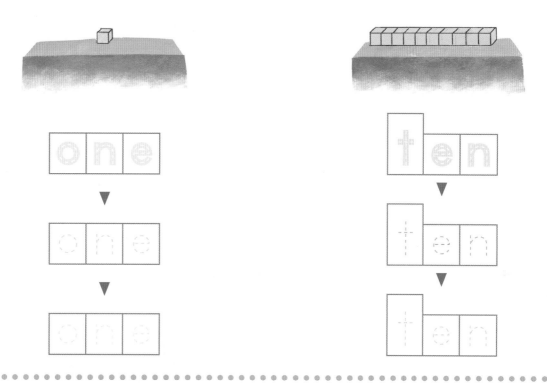

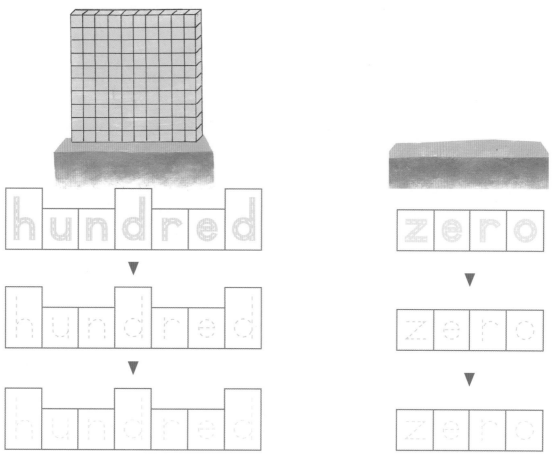

 **Math Words**
Counting

Name

Date

■ Trace each word. Then circle the correct picture.

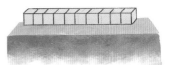

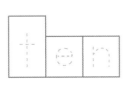

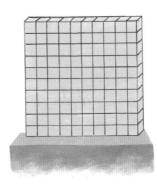

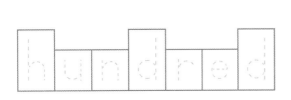

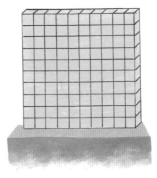

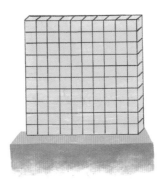

■ Trace and write the letters while saying each word.

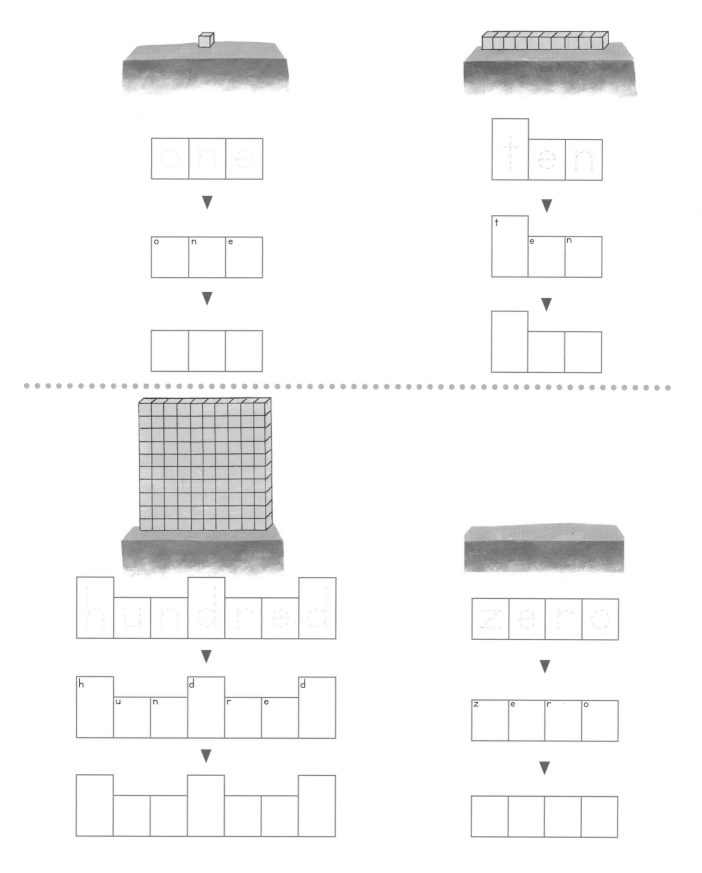

Name

Date

■ Trace the letters while saying each word.

circle

triangle

sides

corners

32

■ Trace the letters while saying each word.

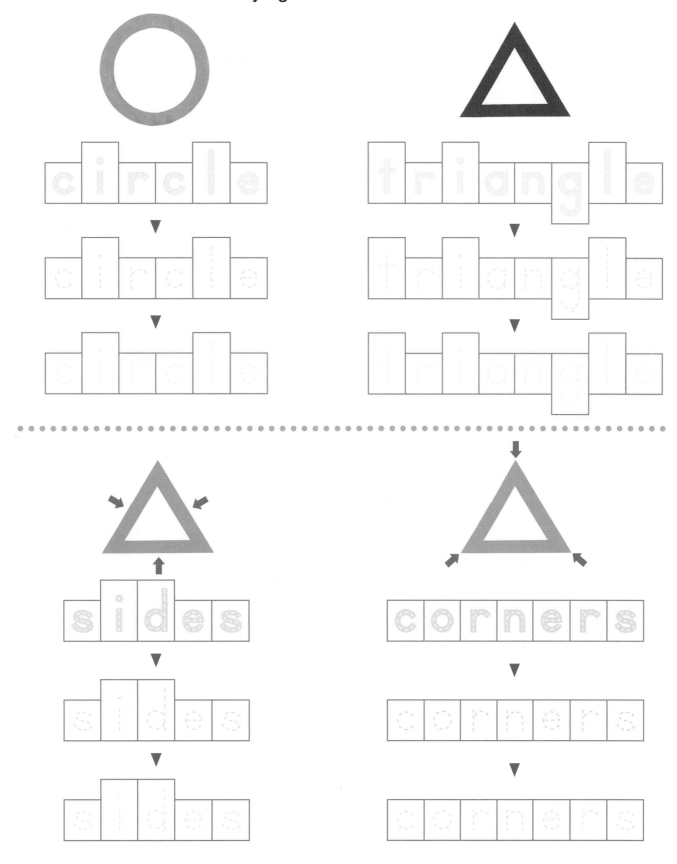

circle

triangle

sides

corners

Math Words
Geometry

Name _____

Date

■ Trace each word. Then circle the correct picture.

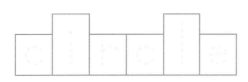

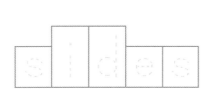

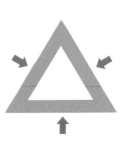

34

■ Trace and write the letters while saying each word.

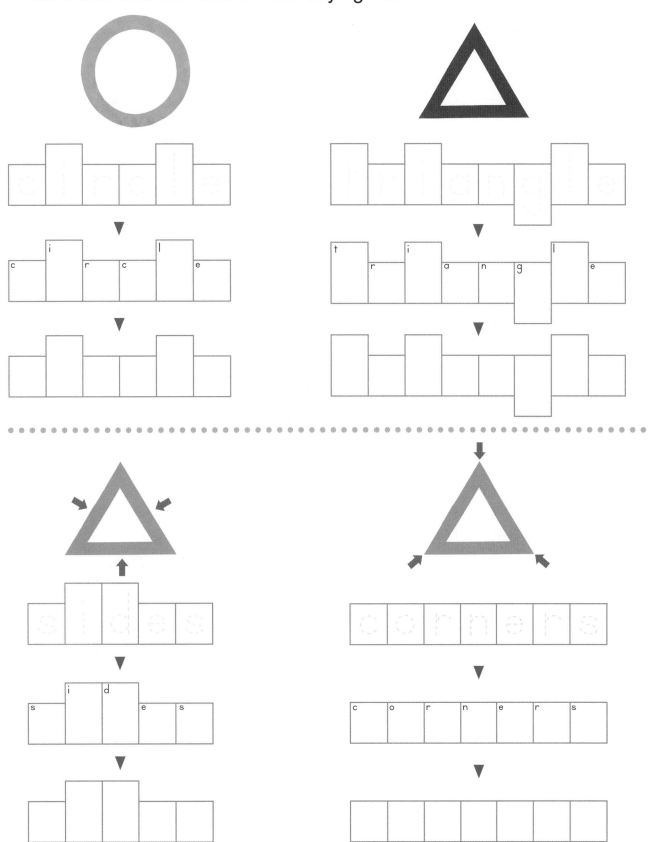

Math Words
Review

Name

Date

■ Write the letters while saying each word.

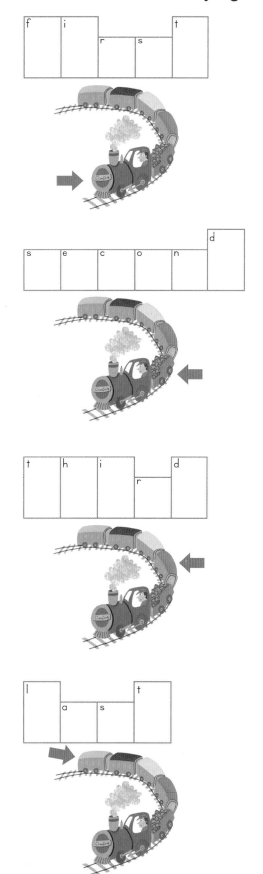

36

■ Write the letters while saying each word.

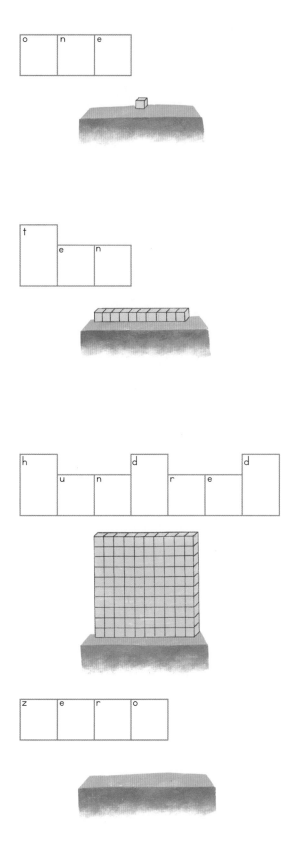

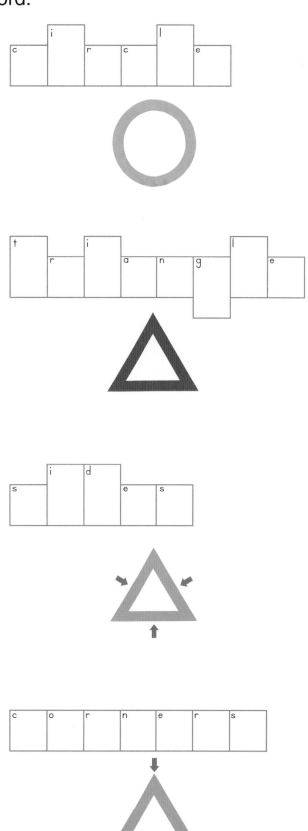

Social Studies Words

Places

Name

Date

■ Trace the letters while saying each word.

park

school

store

airport

To parents/guardians:
In this section, your child will be introduced to reading and writing important words used in social studies. The pictures will help your child understand the meaning of each word.

■ Trace the letters while saying each word.

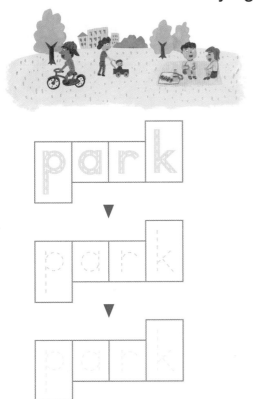

park

▼

park

▼

park

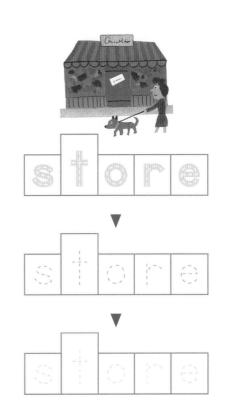

store

▼

store

▼

store

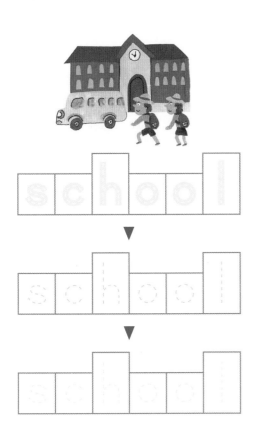

school

▼

school

▼

school

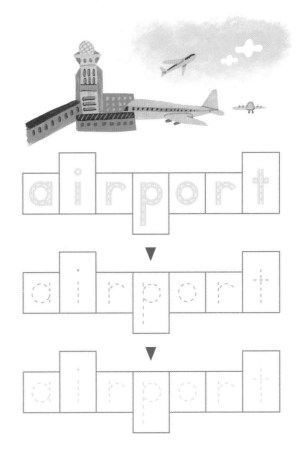

airport

▼

airport

▼

airport

39

Social Studies Words
Places

Name

Date

■ Trace each word. Then match each word with the correct picture.

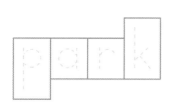 park   ●   ★

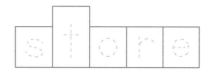 store   ●   ★

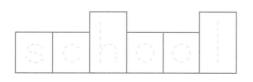 school   ●   ★

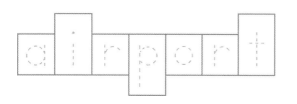 airport   ●   ★

■ Trace and write the letters while saying each word.

p a r k

p a r k

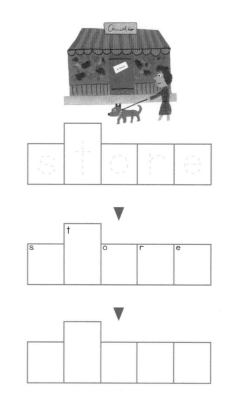

s t o r e

s t o r e

s c h o o l

s c h o o l

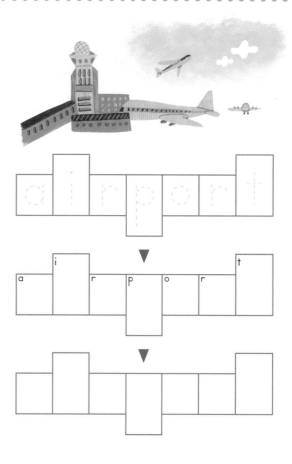

a i r p o r t

a i r p o r t

Social Studies Words
Maps

Name

Date

■ Trace the letters while saying each word.

water

land

map

legend

Legend
school
park
store
airport

42

■ Trace the letters while saying each word.

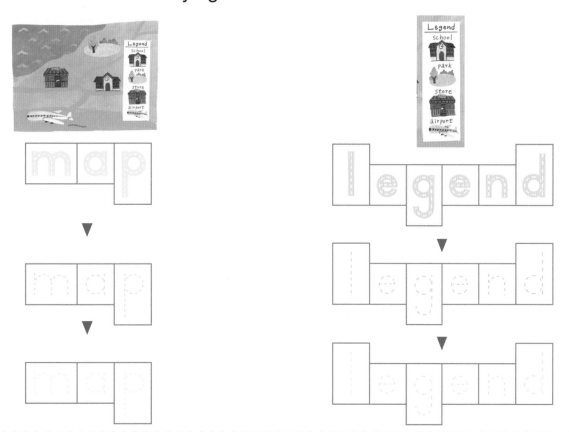

map

▼

map

▼

map

legend

▼

legend

▼

legend

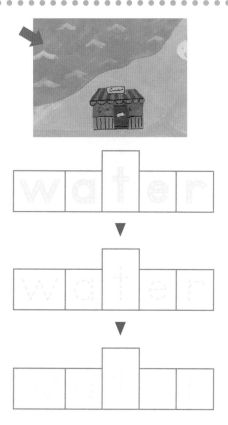

water

▼

water

▼

water

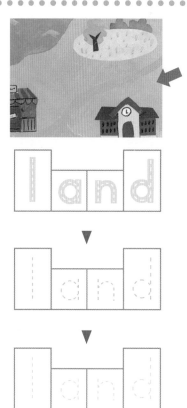

land

▼

land

▼

land

Social Studies Words
Maps

Name

Date

■ Trace each word. Then circle the correct picture.

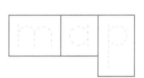

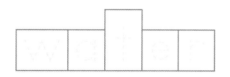

■ Trace and write the letters while saying each word.

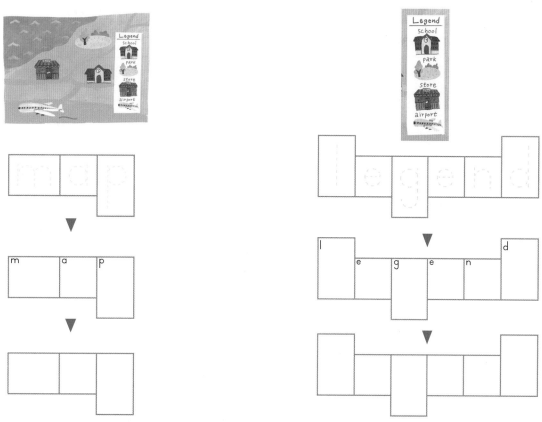

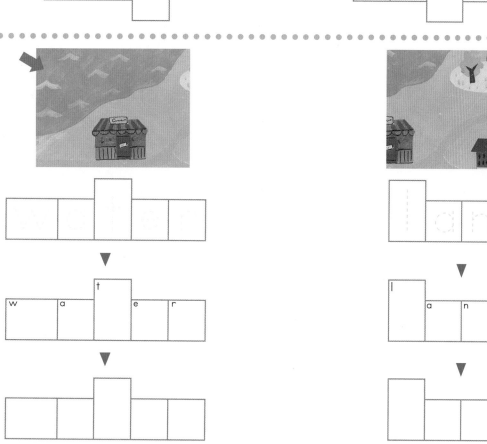

Social Studies Words
Jobs

Name

Date

■ Trace the letters while saying each word.

judge

baker

doctor

artist

■ Trace the letters while saying each word.

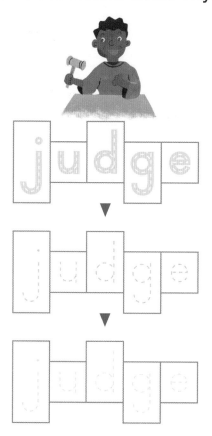

judge

▼

judge

▼

judge

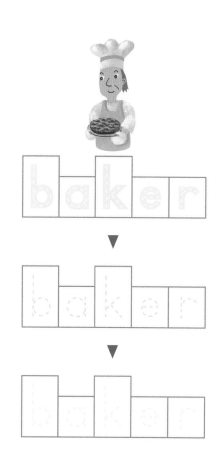

baker

▼

baker

▼

baker

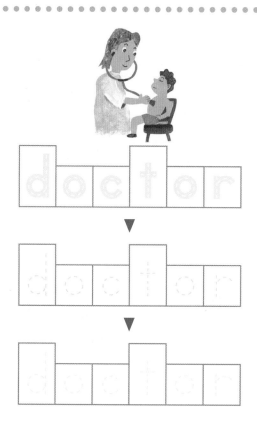

doctor

▼

doctor

▼

doctor

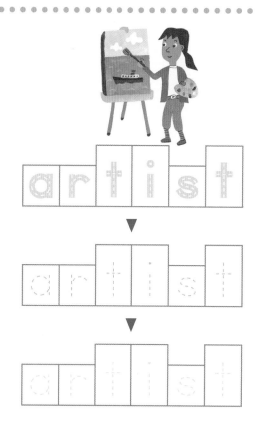

artist

▼

artist

▼

artist

Name

Date

■ Trace each word. Then circle the correct picture.

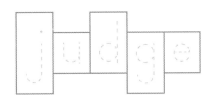

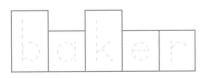

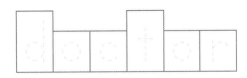

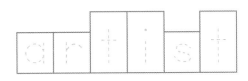

■ Trace and write the letters while saying each word.

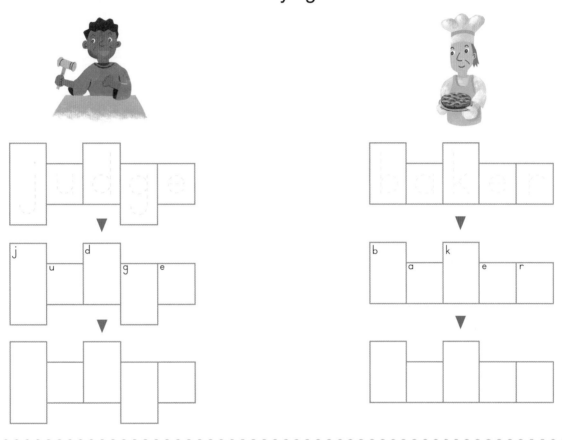

j u d g e

▼

▼

b a k e r

▼

▼

d o c t o r

▼

▼

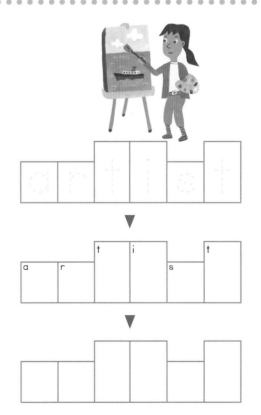

a r t i s t

▼

▼

25 Social Studies Words
The Calendar

Name

Date

■ Trace the letters while saying each word.

day

week

month

year

■ Trace the letters while saying each word.

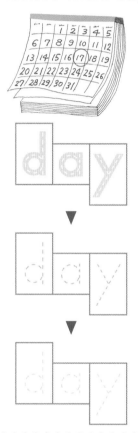

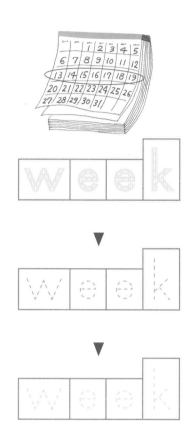

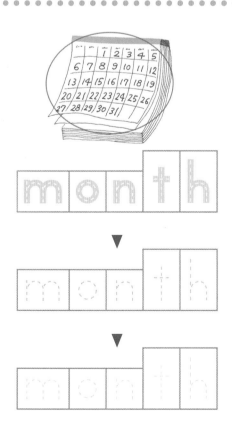

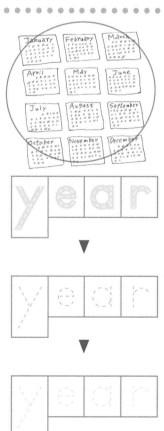

■ Trace each word. Then match each word with the correct picture.

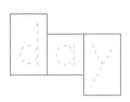 ● ★

 ● ★

 ● ★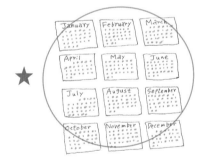

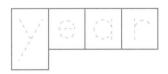 ● ★

▪ Trace and write the letters while saying each word.

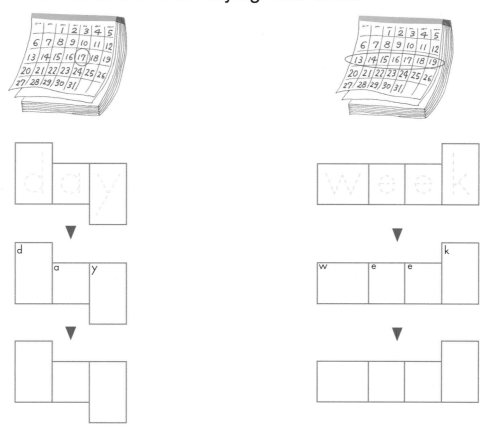

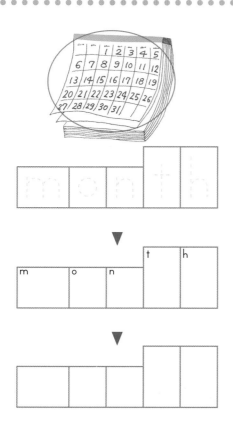

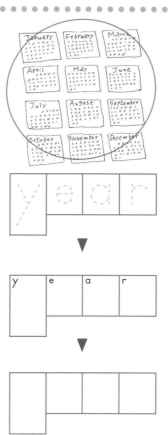

Name

Date

■ Write the letters while saying each word.

k
p	a	r

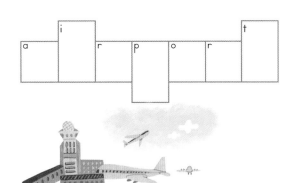

t
s	o	r	e

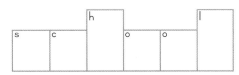

h		l
s	c	o	o

i		t
a	r	p	o	r

| m | a | p |

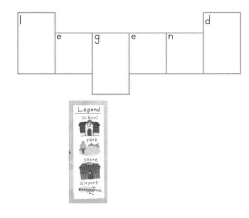

l			d
e	g	e	n

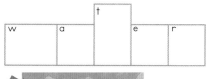

t
w	a	e	r

l		d
a	n

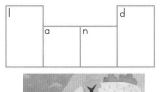

54

■ Write the letters while saying each word.

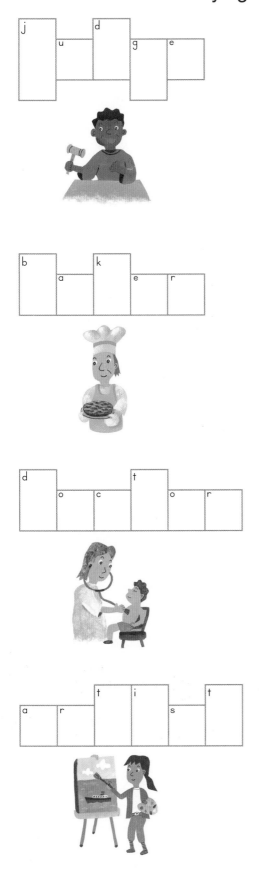

j u d g e

b a k e r

d o c t o r

a r t i s t

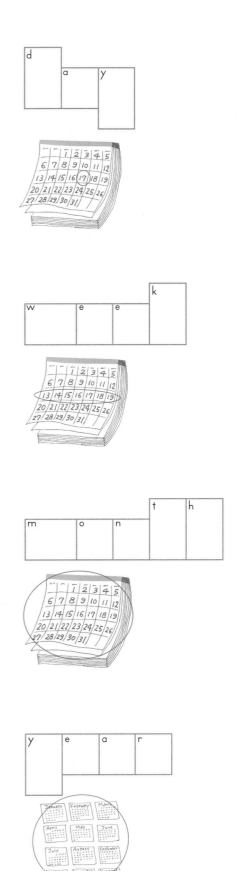

d a y

w e e k

m o n t h

y e a r

55

28 Language Arts Words
Story Time

■ Trace the letters while saying each word.

book

poem

play

movie

To parents/guardians:
In this section, your child will be introduced to reading and writing important words used in language arts. The pictures will help your child understand the meaning of each word.

■ Trace the letters while saying each word.

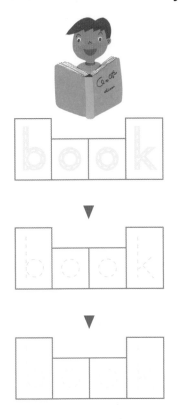

book

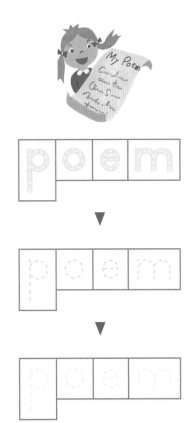

poem

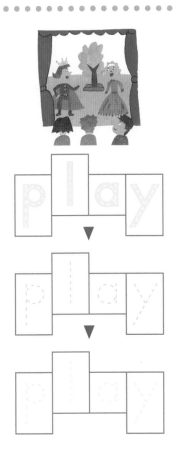

play

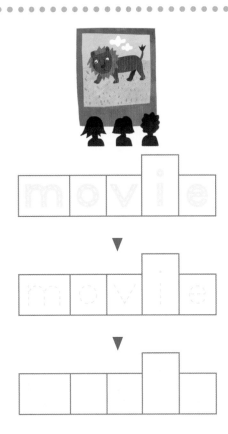

movie

Name

Date

■ Trace each word. Then circle the correct picture.

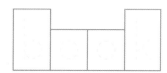

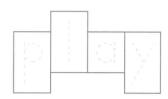

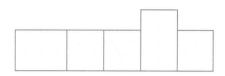

■ Trace and write the letters while saying each word.

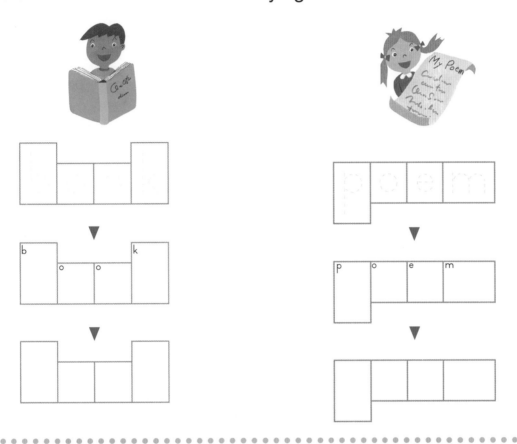

b o o k

p o e m

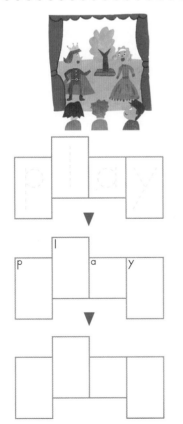

p l a y

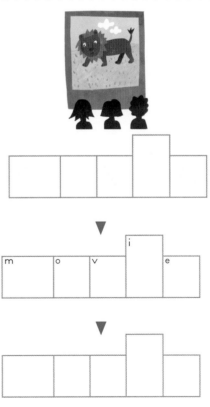

m o v i e

■ Trace the letters while saying each word.

what

who

when

where

■ Trace the letters while saying each word.

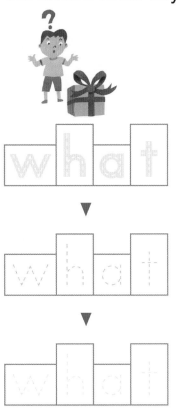

what

▼

what

▼

what

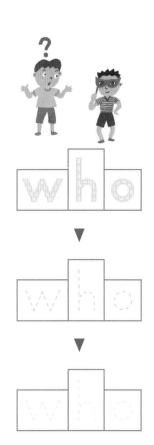

who

▼

who

▼

who

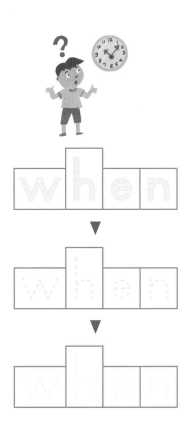

when

▼

when

▼

when

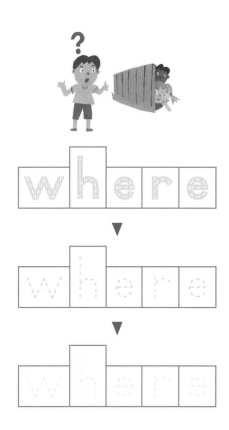

where

▼

where

▼

where

Language Arts Words
Question Words

■ Trace each word. Then match each word with the correct picture.

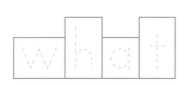   ●   ★

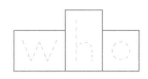   ●   ★

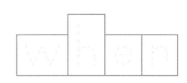   ●   ★

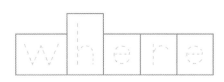   ●   ★

■ Trace and write the letters while saying each word.

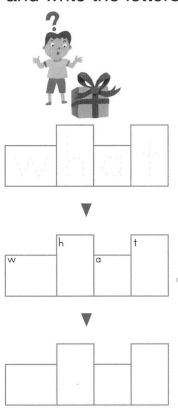

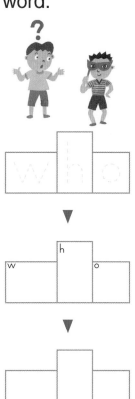

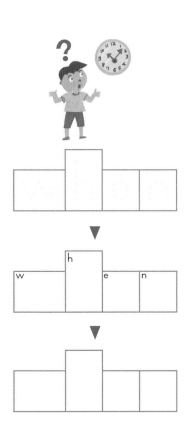

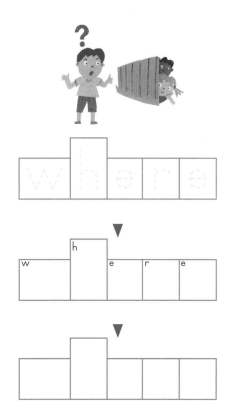

Name

Date

■ Write the letters while saying each word.

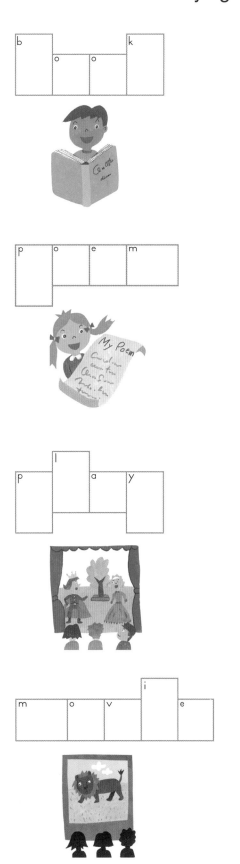

b | o | o | k

p | o | e | m

l
p | a | y

i
m | o | v | e

h | t
w | a

h
w | o

h
w | e | n

h
w | e | r | e

To parents/guardians:
This is the last page of this section before the final review. As an added challenge, the words on this page now appear in a mixed-up order. If your child has difficulty, help them focus on one word at a time.

■ Write the letters while saying each word.

65

Name

Date

■ Write the letters while saying each word.

s | u | | n

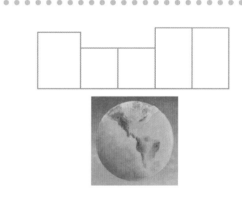

m | o | o | n

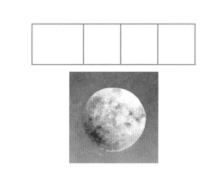

E | | t | h
| a | r |

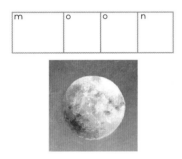

t
s | | a | r

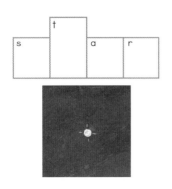

■ Write the letters while saying each word.

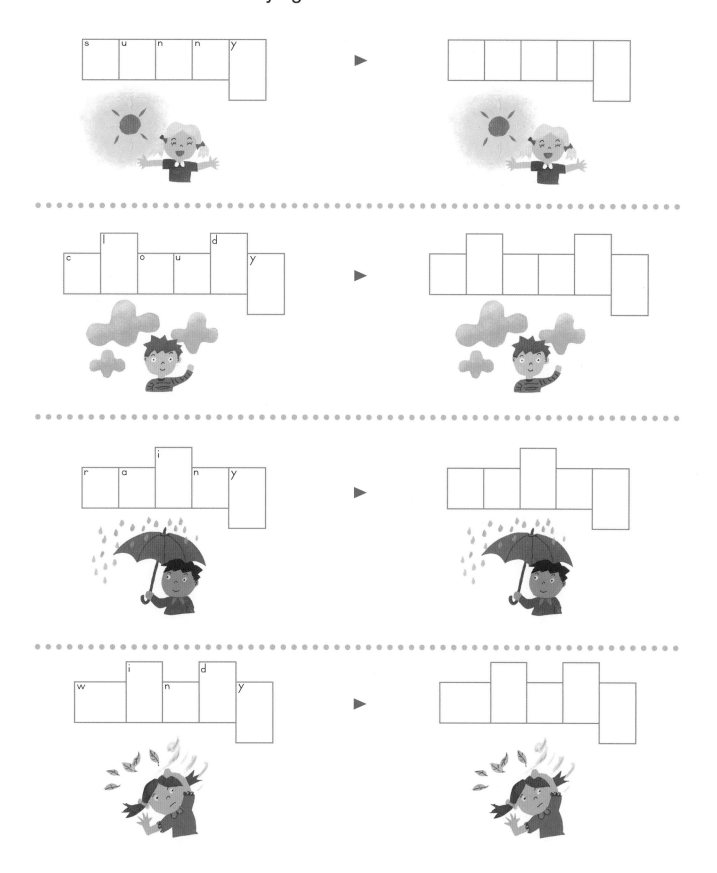

Review

Science Words

Name

Date

■ Write the letters while saying each word.

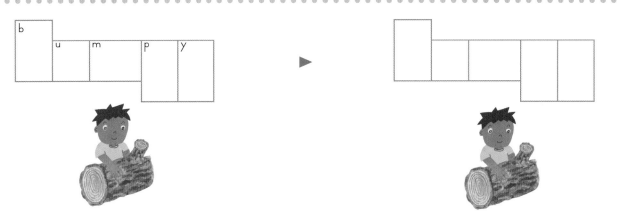

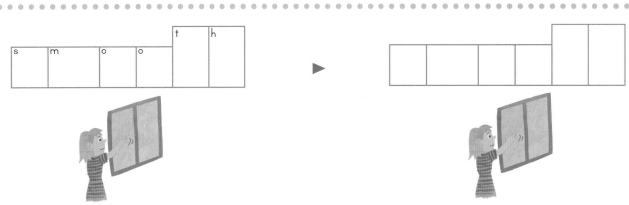

■ Write the letters while saying each word.

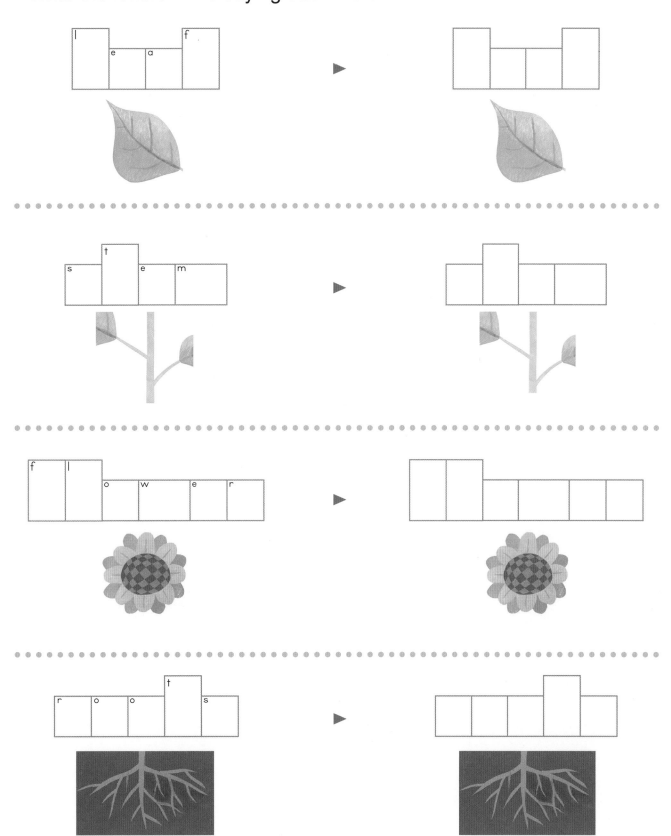

Name

Date

■ Write the letters while saying each word.

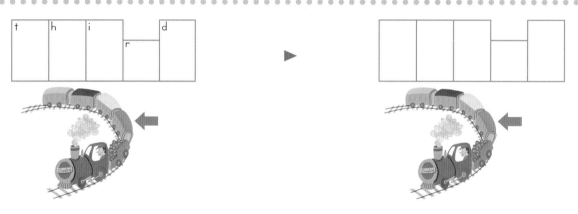

70

■ Write the letters while saying each word.

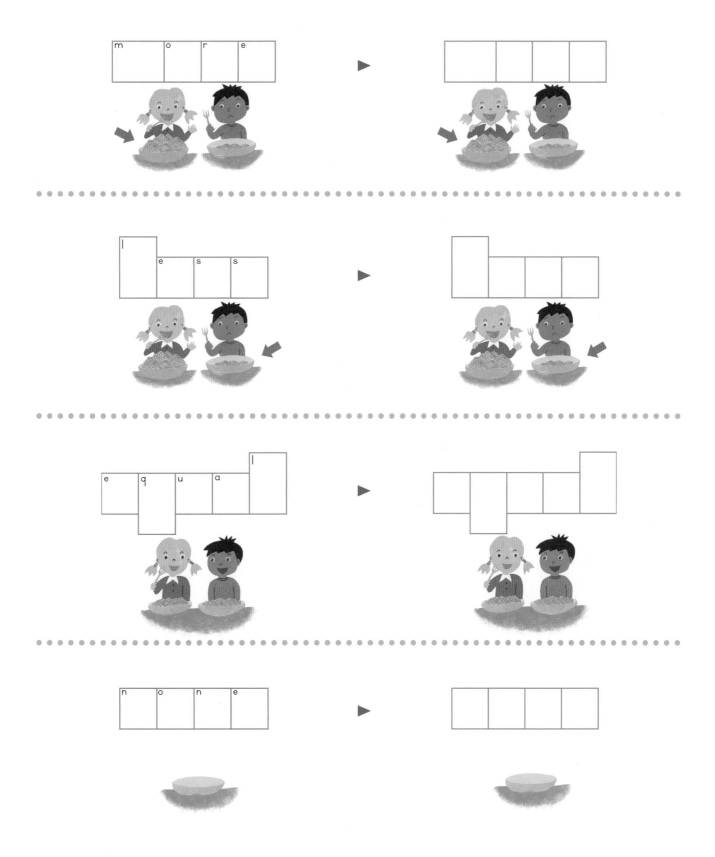

Review
Math Words

Name

Date

■ Write the letters while saying each word.

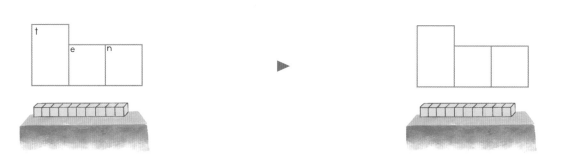

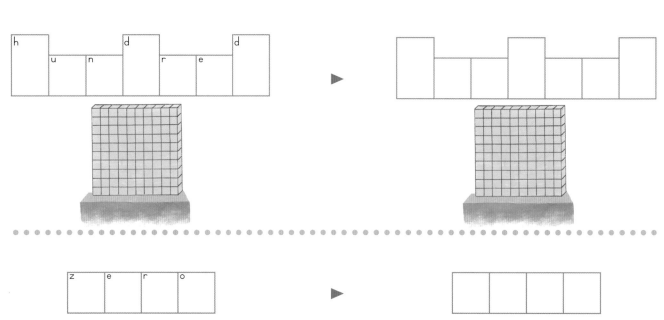

72

■ Write the letters while saying each word.

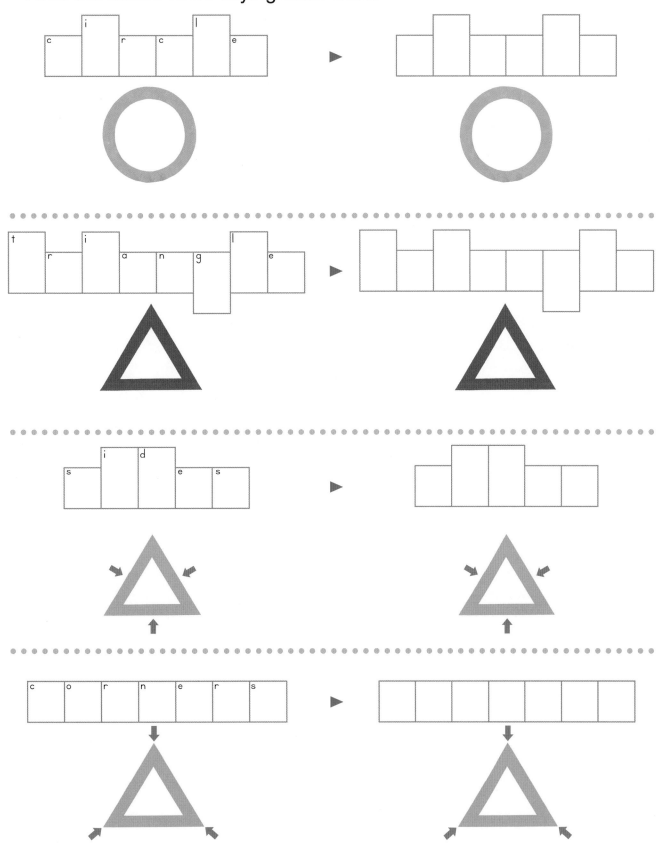

37 Review
Social Studies Words

■ Write the letters while saying each word.

p | a | r | k

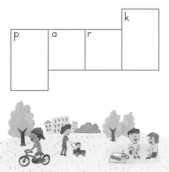 

s | t | o | r | e

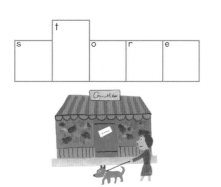 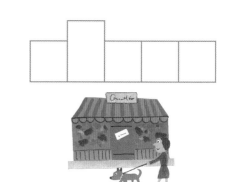

s | c | h | o | o | l

  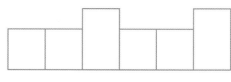

a | i | r | p | o | r | t

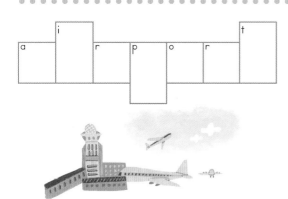 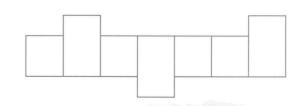 

▦ Write the letters while saying each word.

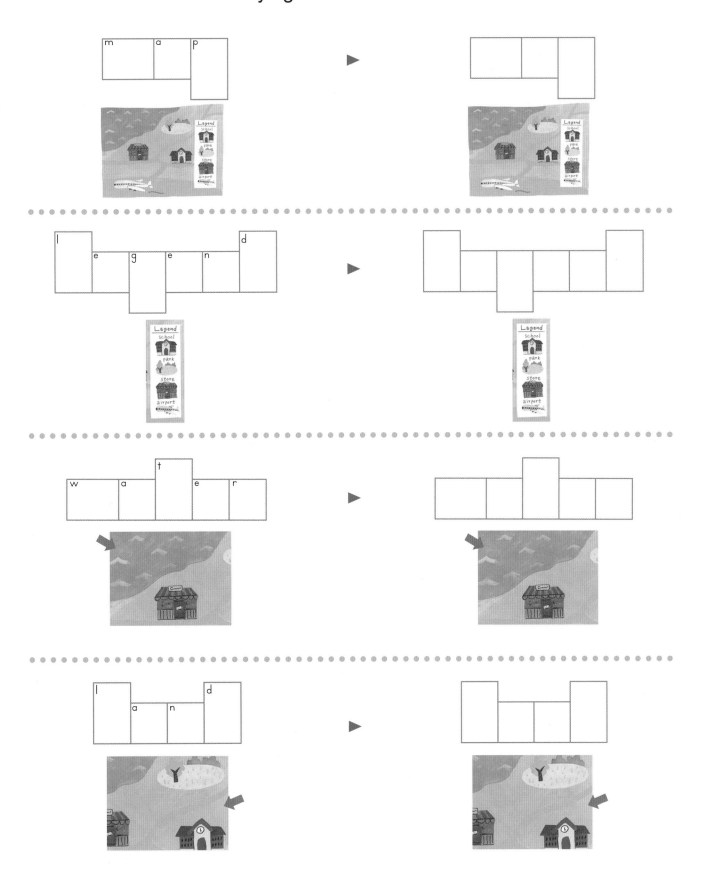

Name

Date

■ Write the letters while saying each word.

j | d | | |
u | | g | e |

b | k | | |
a | | e | r |

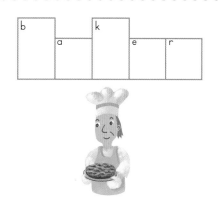

d | t | | |
o | c | | o | r |

| t | i | t |
a | r | | s | |

■ Write the letters while saying each word.

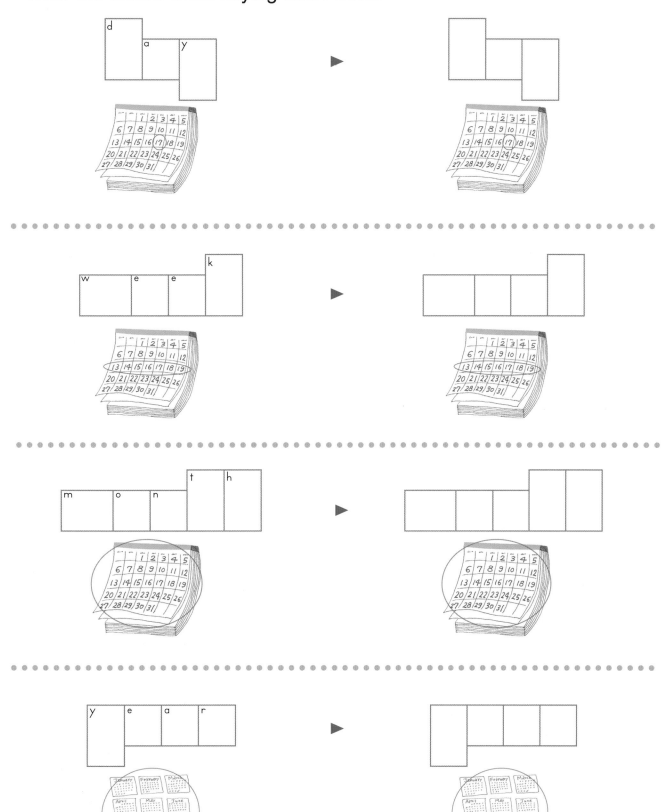

Name

Date

■ Write the letters while saying each word.

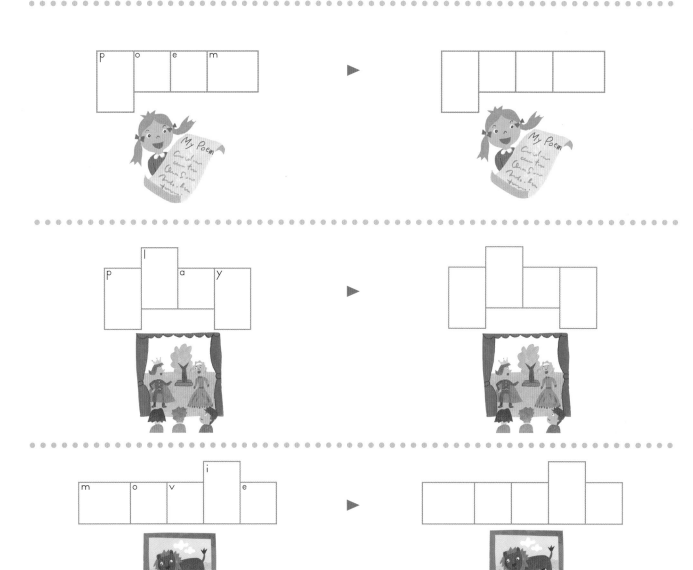

To parents/guardians:
This is the last exercise of this section. Please praise
your child for the effort it took to complete this section.

■ Write the letters while saying each word.

My First WORDS for SCHOOL

Part 2

Table of Contents

■ Trace the letters while saying each word.

spring

summer

fall

winter

To parents/guardians:
In this section, your child will be introduced to reading and writing a new group of important words used in science. The pictures will help your child understand the meaning of each word.

■ Trace the letters while saying each word.

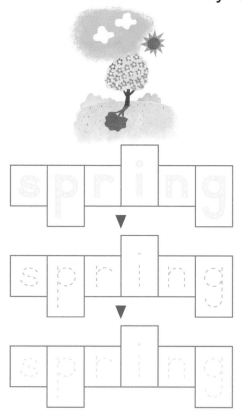

spring

▼

spring

▼

spring

summer

▼

summer

▼

summer

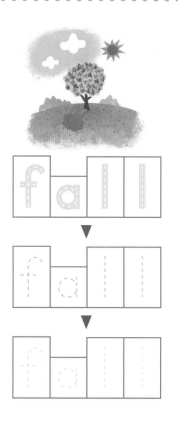

fall

▼

fall

▼

fall

winter

▼

winter

▼

winter

Science Words

Seasons

 Name _____

Date _____

■ Trace each word. Then circle the correct picture.

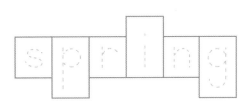

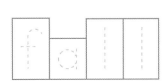

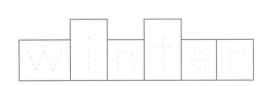

84

■ Trace and write the letters while saying each word.

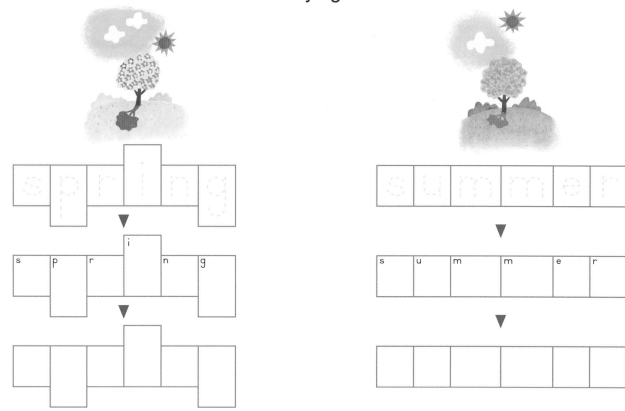

spring

s p r i n g

summer

s u m m e r

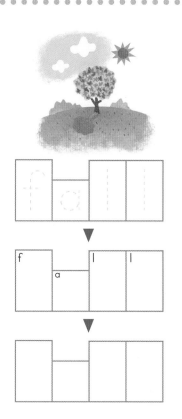

fall

f a l l

winter

w i n t e r

Name

Date

■ Trace the letters while saying each word.

pushing

pulling

rolling

ramp

To parents/guardians:
Your child may need your help reading each word aloud at first.
This book provides plenty of practice and repetition, so your
child can eventually learn to read each word on their own.

■ Trace the letters while saying each word.

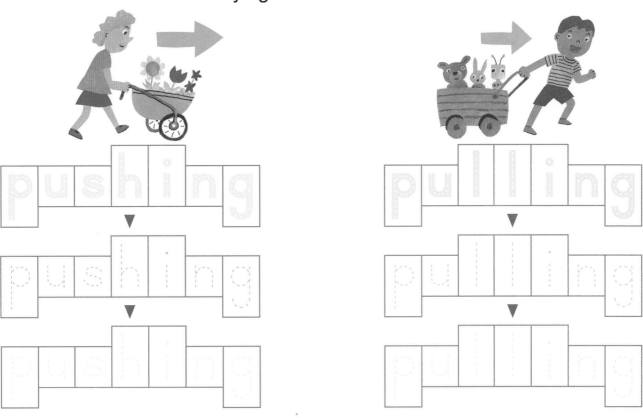

pushing

pulling

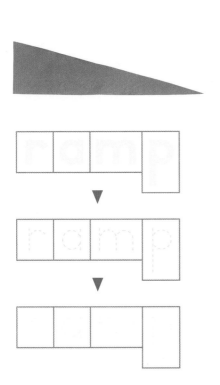

ramp

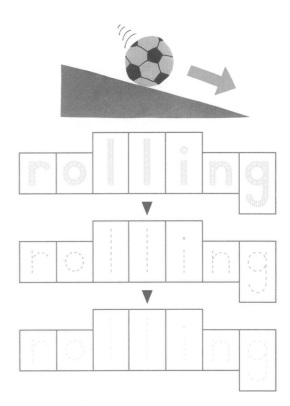

rolling

Science Words
Force and Motion

Name

Date

■ Trace each word. Then circle the correct picture.

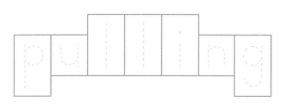

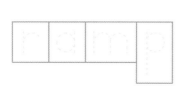

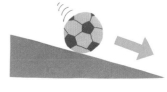

■ Trace and write the letters while saying each word.

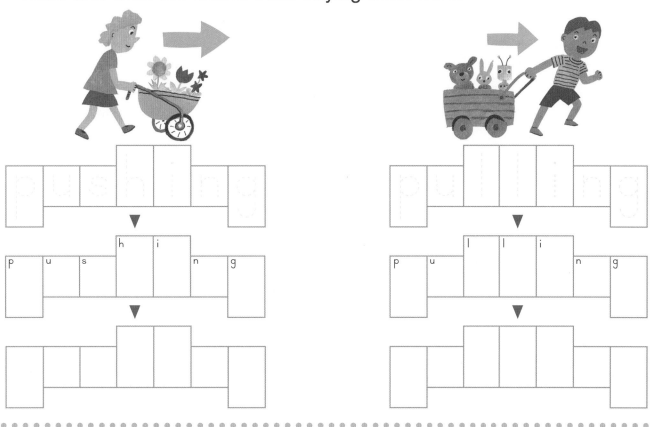

pushing

| p | u | s | h | i | n | g |

pulling

| p | u | l | l | i | n | g |

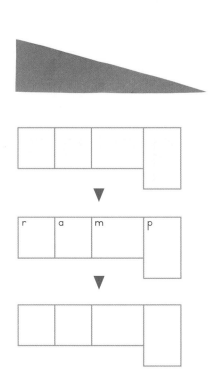

ramp

| r | a | m | p |

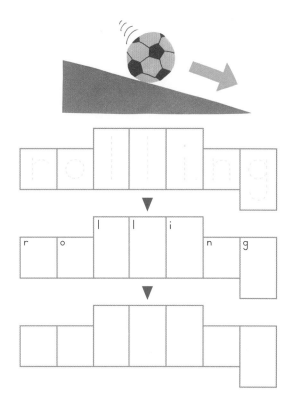

rolling

| r | o | l | l | i | n | g |

Science Words
Energy and Its Effects

Name

Date

■ Trace the letters while saying each word.

■ Trace the letters while saying each word.

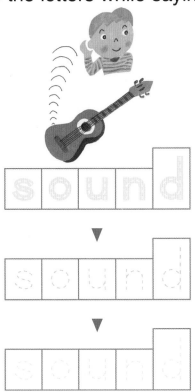

sound

▼

sound

▼

sound

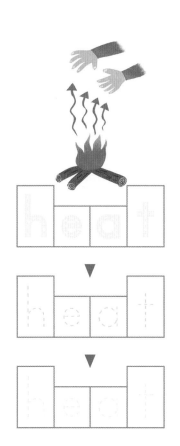

heat

▼

heat

▼

heat

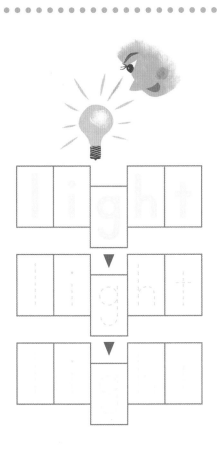

light

▼

light

▼

light

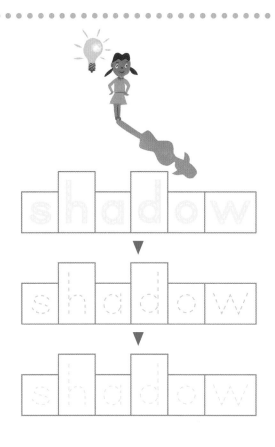

shadow

▼

shadow

▼

shadow

Science Words
Energy and Its Effects

Name _____

Date _____

■ Trace each word. Then match each word with the correct picture.

   ●   ★

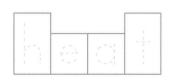   ●   ★

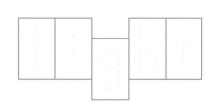   ●   ★

   ●   ★

92

■Trace and write the letters while saying each word.

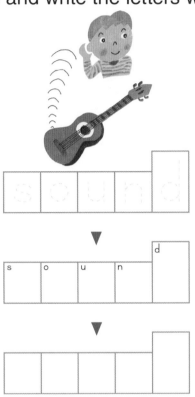

s o u n d

▼

s o u n d

▼

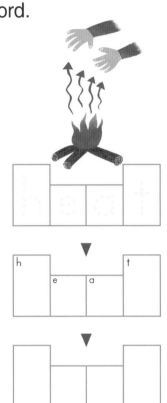

h e a t

▼

h e a t

▼

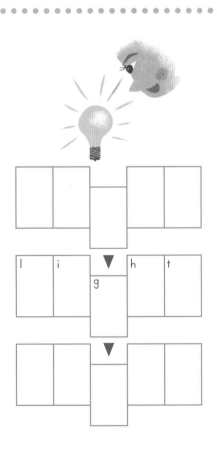

l i g h t

▼

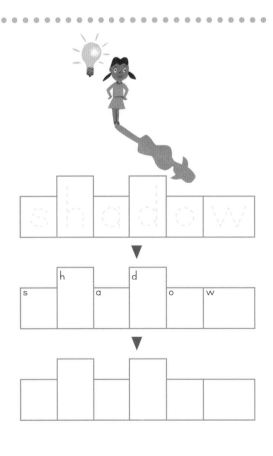

s h a d o w

▼

s h a d o w

▼

93

Science Words

Types of Animals

■ Trace the letters while saying each word.

fish

insects

reptiles

mammals

94

■ Trace the letters while saying each word.

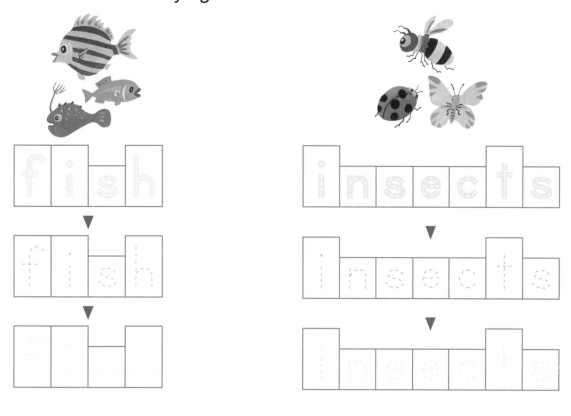

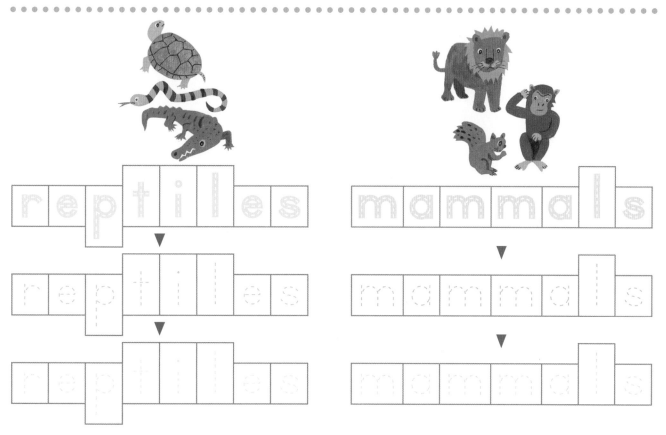

95

Science Words
Types of Animals

■ Trace each word. Then match each word with the correct picture.

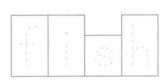　　●　　★　

　　●　　★　

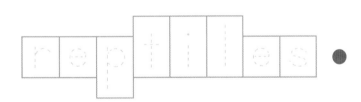　　●　　★　

　　●　　★　

■ Trace and write the letters while saying each word.

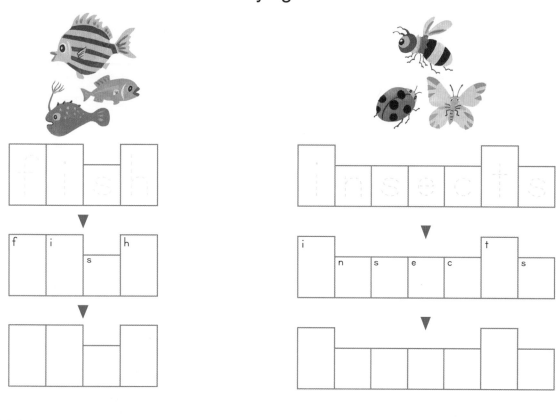

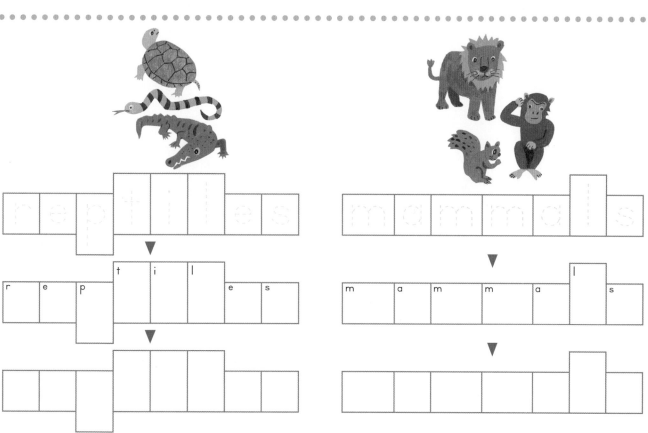

Name

Date

■ Write the letters while saying each word.

98

■ Write the letters while saying each word.

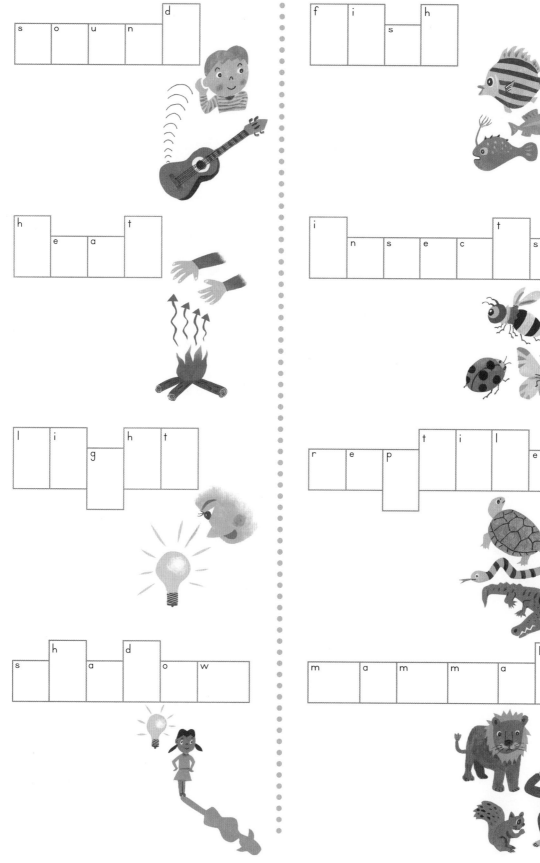

| s | o | u | n | d |

| f | i | | h |
| | | s | |

| h | | | t |
| | e | a | |

| i | | | t |
| | n | s | e | c | s |

| l | i | | h | t |
| | | g | | |

| | | t | i | l | |
| r | e | p | | | e | s |

| | h | | d |
| s | | a | | o | w |

| | | | l |
| m | a | m | m | a | | s |

99

Math Words
Measurement

Name

Date

■ Trace the letters while saying each word.

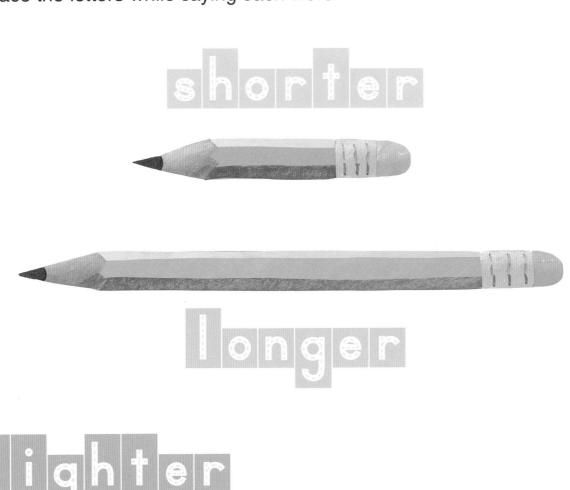

shorter

longer

lighter

heavier

To parents/guardians:
In this section, your child will be introduced to reading and writing
a new group of important words used in math. The pictures will
help your child understand the meaning of each word.

■ Trace the letters while saying each word.

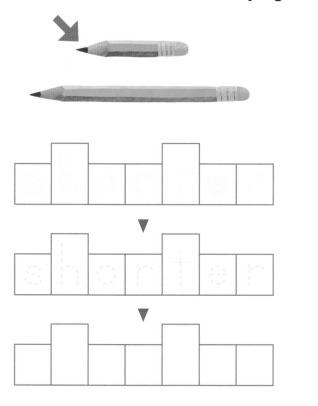

shorter

▼

shorter

▼

shorter

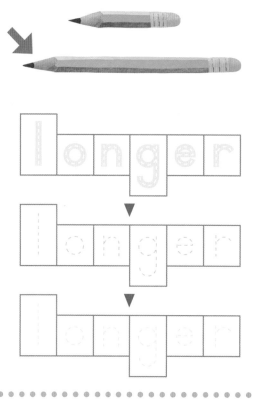

longer

▼

longer

▼

longer

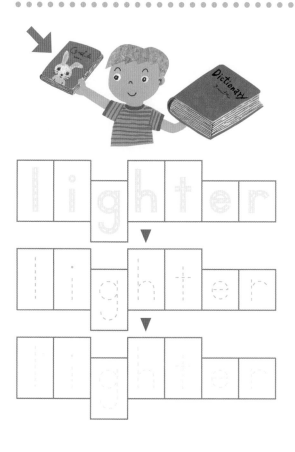

lighter

▼

lighter

▼

lighter

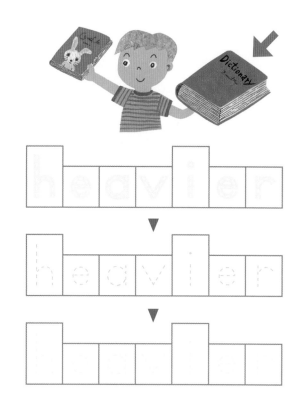

heavier

▼

heavier

▼

heavier

Math Words
Measurement

■ Trace each word. Then match each word with the correct picture.

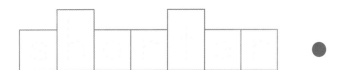   ●

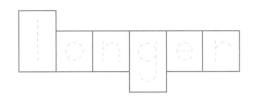   ●

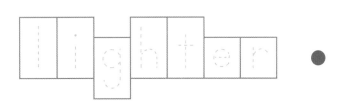   ●

   ●

■ Trace and write the letters while saying each word.

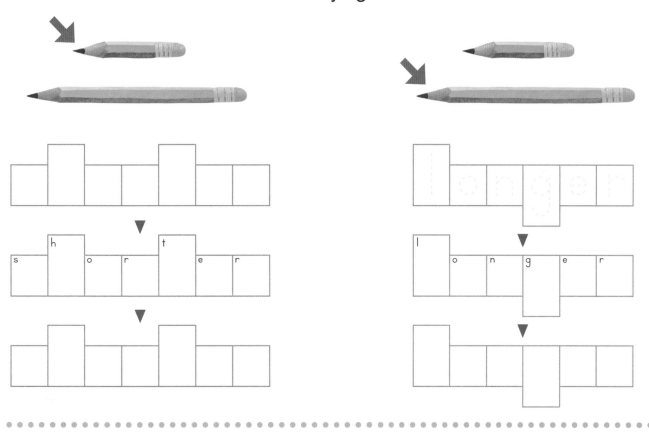

shorter

longer

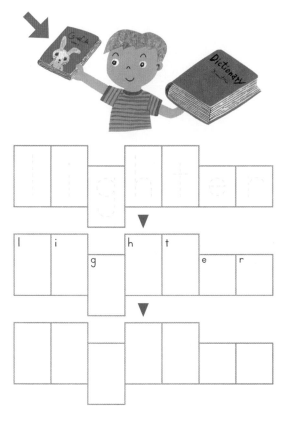

lighter

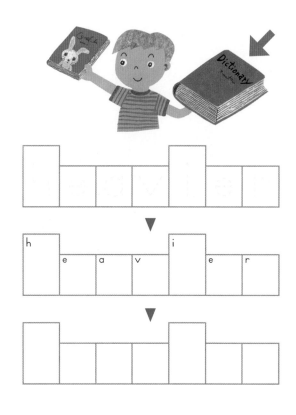

heavier

Name

Date

■ Trace the letters while saying each word.

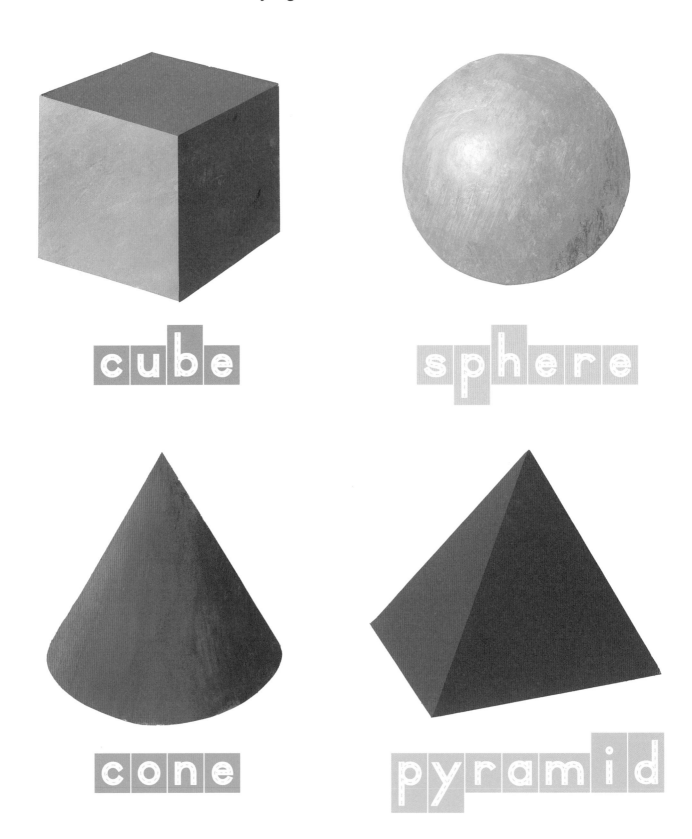

cube

sphere

cone

pyramid

■ Trace the letters while saying each word.

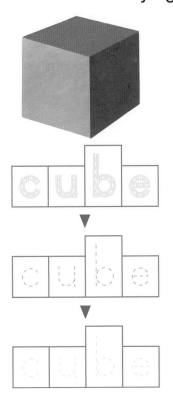

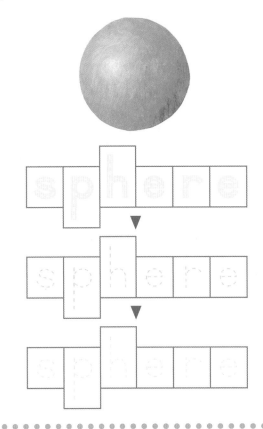

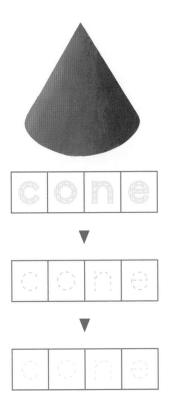

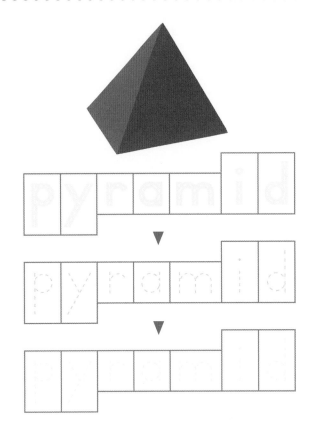

 **Math Words**
Solids

Name

Date

■ Trace each word. Then circle the correct picture.

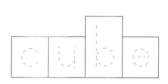

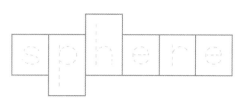

■ Trace and write the letters while saying each word.

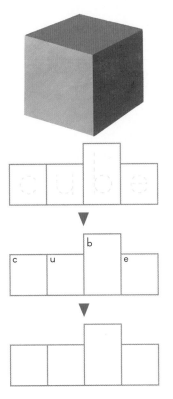

c u b e

b
c u e

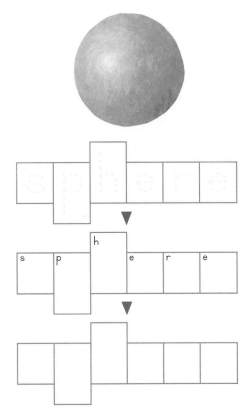

s p h e r e

h
s p e r e

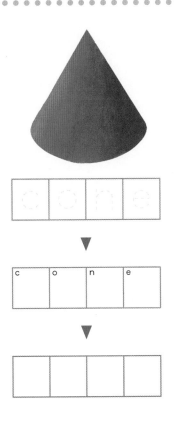

c o n e

c o n e

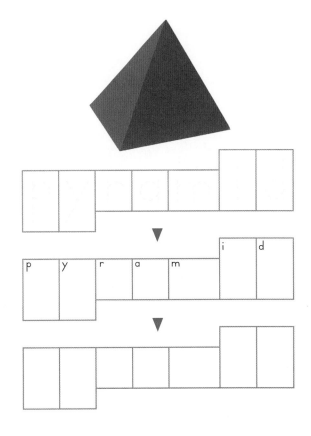

i d
p y r a m

Math Words
Fractions

Name

Date

■ Trace the letters while saying each word.

whole

halves

thirds

fourths

■ Trace the letters while saying each word.

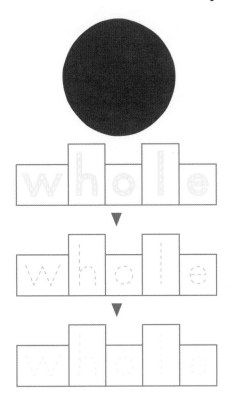

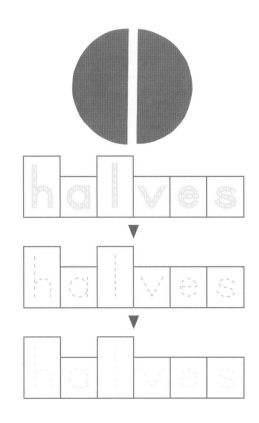

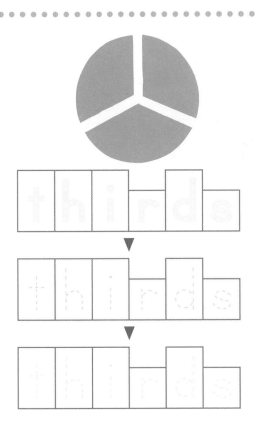

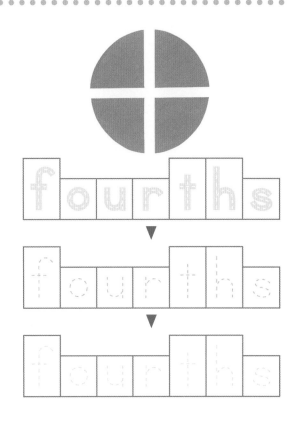

Math Words
Fractions

Name

Date

■ Trace each word. Then circle the correct picture.

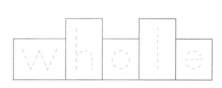  

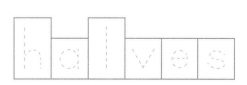 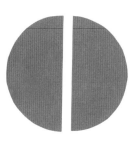 

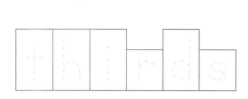  

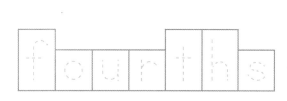 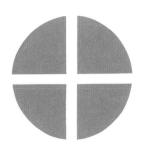 

■ Trace and write the letters while saying each word.

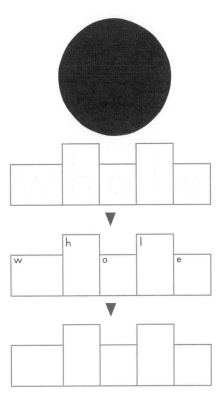

w h o l e

whole

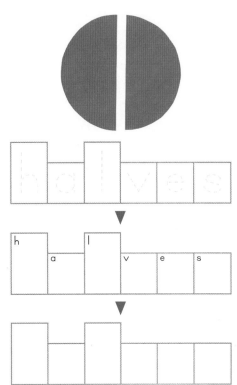

h a l v e s

halves

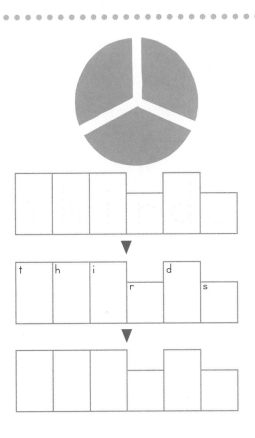

t h i r d s

thirds

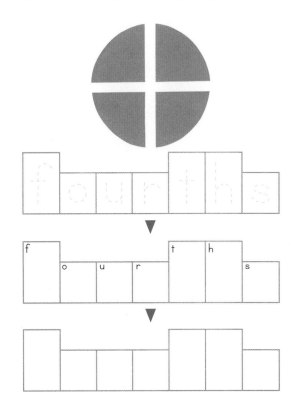

f o u r t h s

fourths

16 Math Words
Review

Name

Date

■ Write the letters while saying each word.

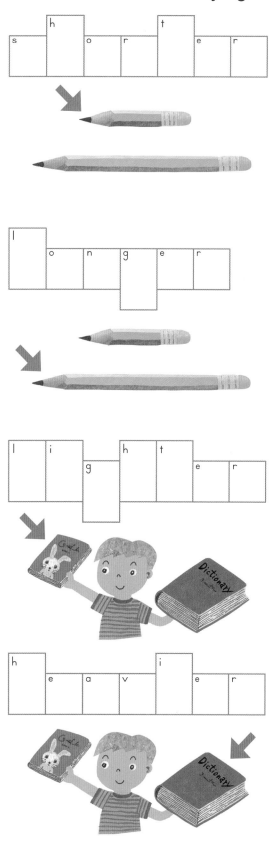

s | h | o | r | t | e | r

l | o | n | g | e | r

l | i | g | h | t | g | e | r

h | e | a | v | i | e | r

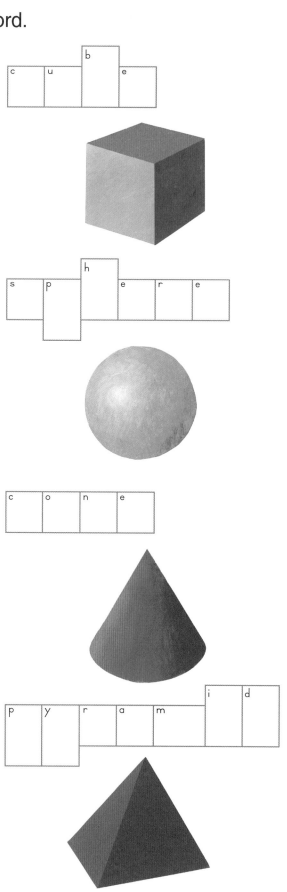

c | u | b | e

s | p | h | e | r | e

c | o | n | e

p | y | r | a | m | i | d

■ Write the letters while saying each word.

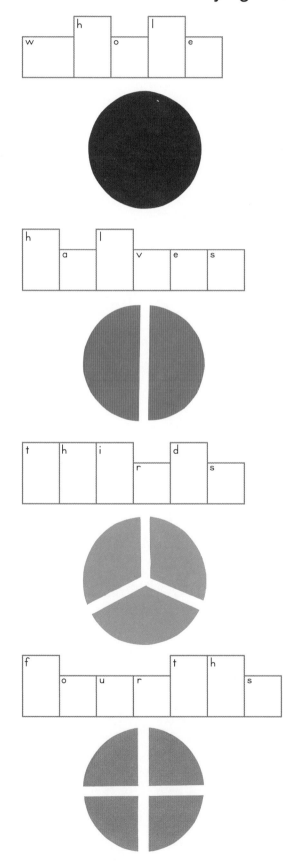

Social Studies Words

Landforms

Name

Date

■ Trace the letters while saying each word.

mountain

hill

river

lake

To parents/guardians:
In this section, your child will be introduced to reading and writing a new group of important words used in social studies. The pictures will help your child understand the meaning of each word.

■ Trace the letters while saying each word.

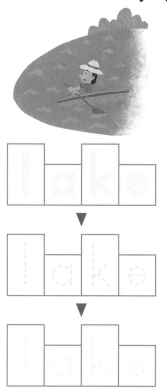

lake

lake

lake

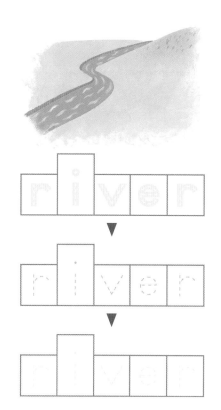

river

river

river

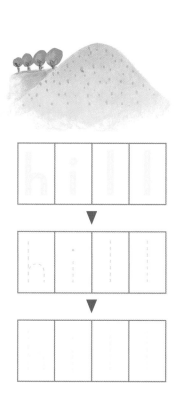

hill

hill

mountain

mountain

mountain

Social Studies Words
Landforms

Name _____

Date _____

■ Trace each word. Then circle the correct picture.

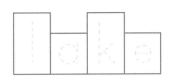  

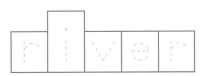  

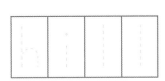  

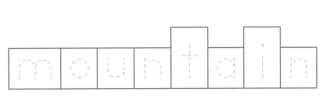  

■ Trace and write the letters while saying each word.

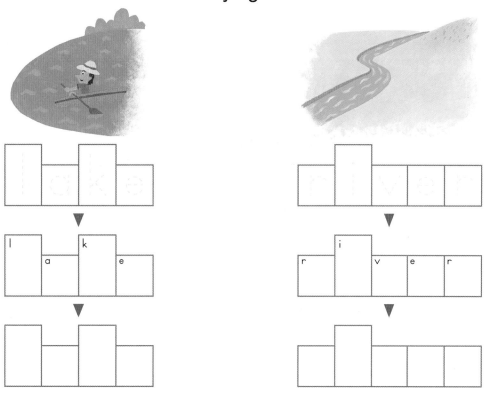

l a k e

▼

l   a   k   e

▼

r i v e r

▼

r   i   v   e   r

▼

h i l l

▼

h   i   l   l

▼

m o u n t a i n

▼

m   o   u   n   t   a   i   n

▼

■ Trace the letters while saying each word.

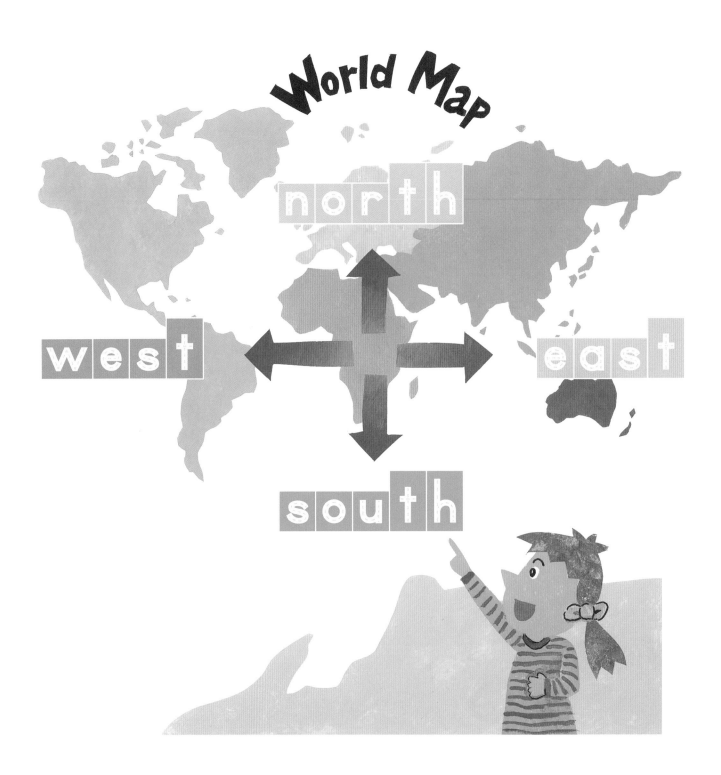

World Map

north

west

east

south

■ Trace the letters while saying each word.

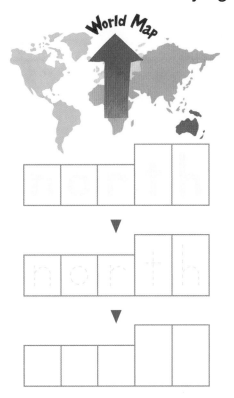

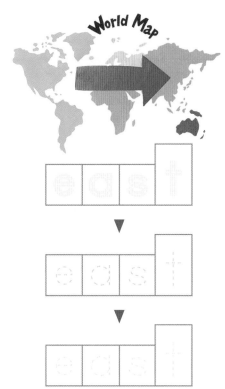

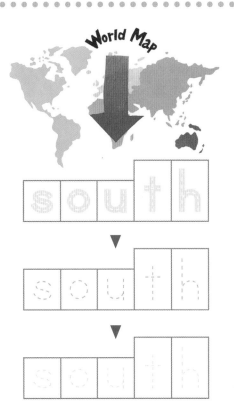

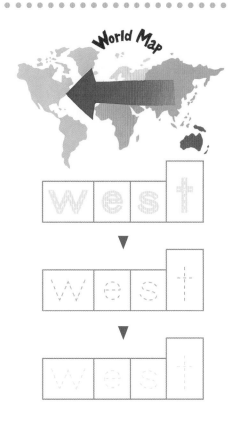

Social Studies Words
Cardinal Directions

■ Trace each word. Then circle the correct picture.

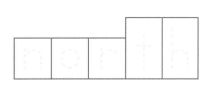

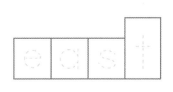

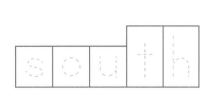

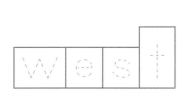

■ Trace and write the letters while saying each word.

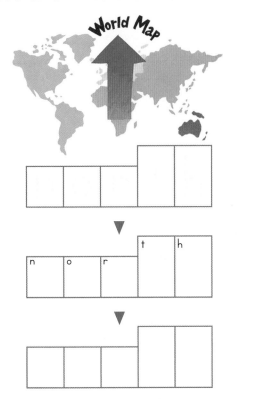

n o r t h

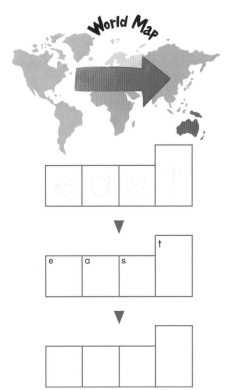

e a s t

e a s t

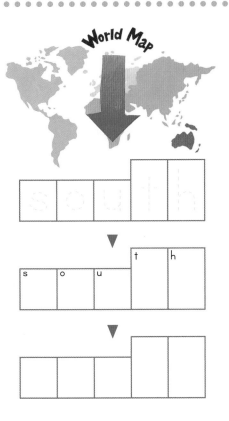

s o u t h

s o u t h

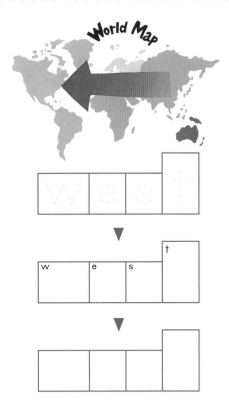

w e s t

w e s t

Social Studies Words

My Needs

Name

Date

■ Trace the letters while saying each word.

food

clothing

shelter

friends

■ Trace the letters while saying each word.

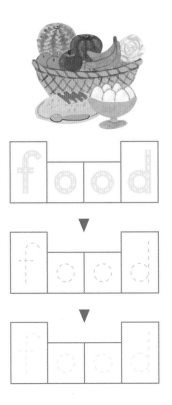

food

food

food

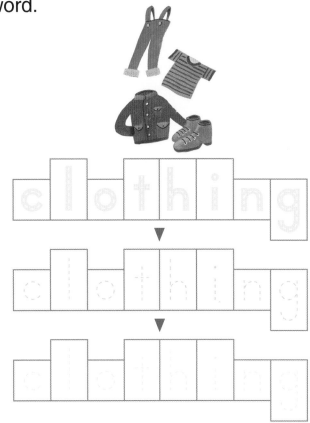

clothing

clothing

clothing

shelter

shelter

shelter

friends

friends

friends

Social Studies Words

My Needs

Name

Date

■ Trace each word. Then match each word with the correct picture.

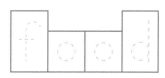 ●

★

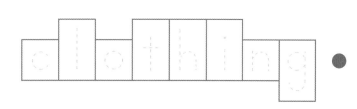 ●

★

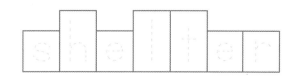 ●

★

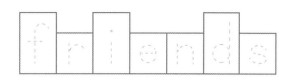 ●

★

■ Trace and write the letters while saying each word.

f o o d

▼

f | | | d
| o | o |

▼

c l o t h i n g

▼

c | l | | t | h | | n | g
| | o | | | | i | |

▼

s h e l t e r

▼

s | h | | l | t | |
| | e | | | e | r

▼

f r i e n d s

▼

f | | i | | | d |
| r | | e | n | | s

▼

Social Studies Words
Economics

■ Trace the letters while saying each word.

needs

wants

money

price

126

■ Trace the letters while saying each word.

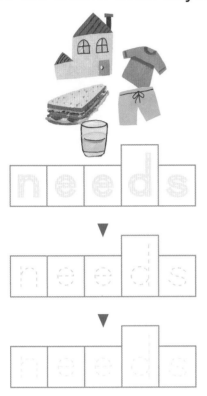

needs

▼

needs

▼

needs

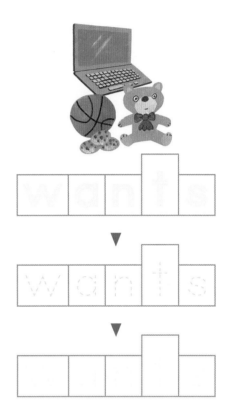

wants

▼

wants

▼

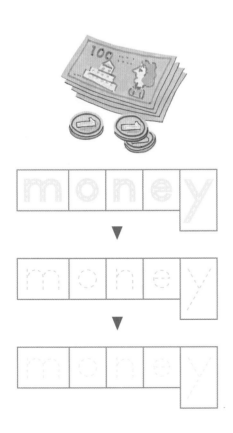

money

▼

money

▼

money

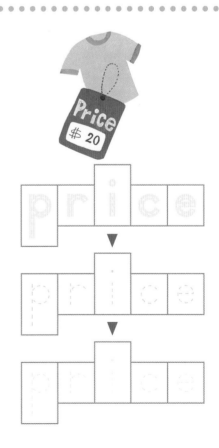

price

▼

price

▼

price

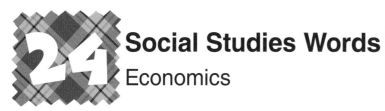

Social Studies Words
Economics

Trace each word. Then match each word with the correct picture.

needs   ●   ★

wants   ●   ★

money   ●   ★

price   ●   ★

■ Trace and write the letters while saying each word.

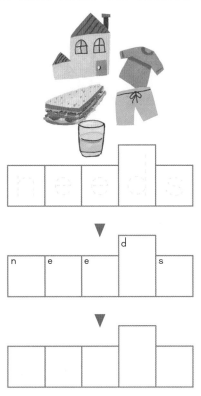

| n | e | e | d | s |

▼

| n | e | e | | d | | s |

▼

| | | | | | |

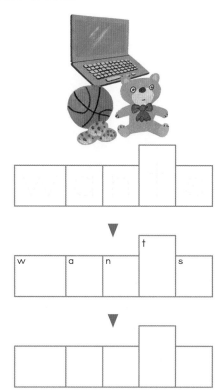

| | | | | |

▼

| w | a | n | | t | | s |

▼

| | | | | | |

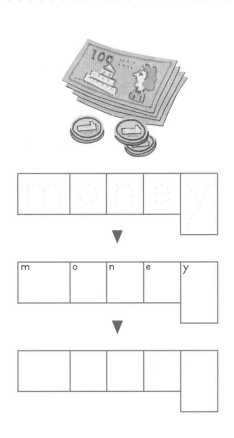

| m | o | n | e | y |

▼

| m | o | n | e | | y |

▼

| | | | | |

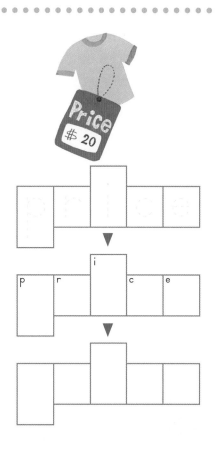

| p | | r | | i | c | e |

▼

| p | r | | i | | c | e |

▼

| | | | | |

Name

Date

■ Write the letters while saying each word.

| l | | k | |
| a | | e | |

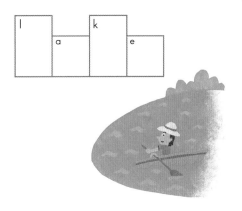

| | i | | | |
| r | v | e | r |

| h | i | l | l |

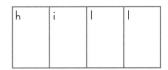

| m | o | u | | t | | a | i | n |

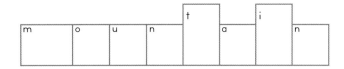

| n | o | r | t | h |

| e | a | s | t |

| s | o | u | t | h |

| w | e | s | t |

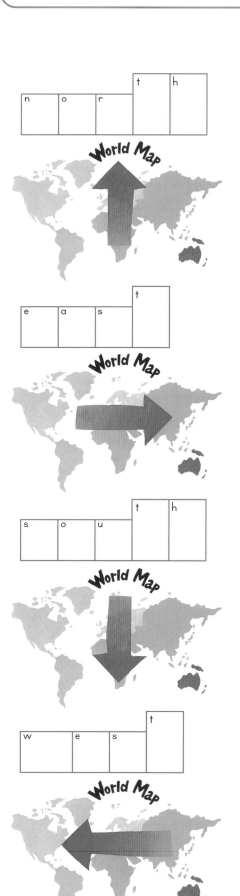

■ Write the letters while saying each word.

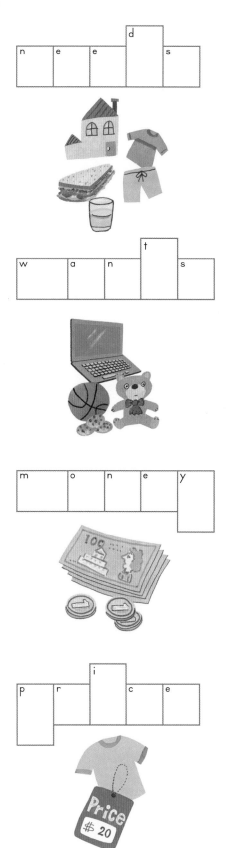

Language Arts Words
Parts of a Book

■ Trace the letters while saying each word.

To parents/guardians:
In this section, your child will be introduced to reading and writing a new group of important words used in language arts. The pictures will help your child understand the meaning of each word.

■ Trace the letters while saying each word.

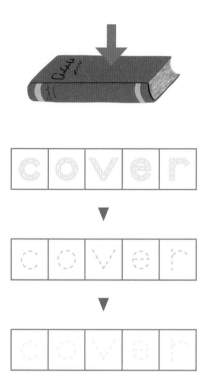

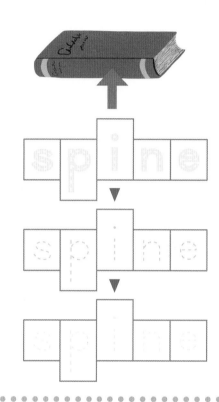

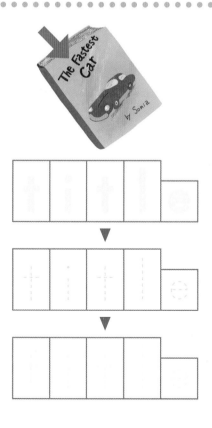

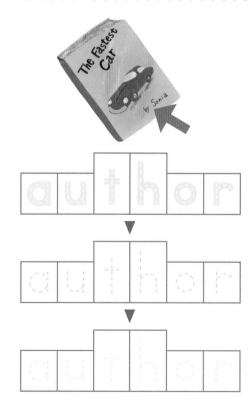

Language Arts Words

Parts of a Book

Name

Date

■ Trace each word. Then circle the correct picture.

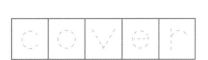  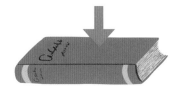

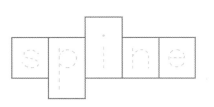 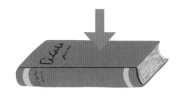 

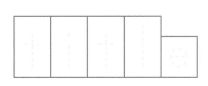  

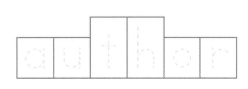  

■ Trace and write the letters while saying each word.

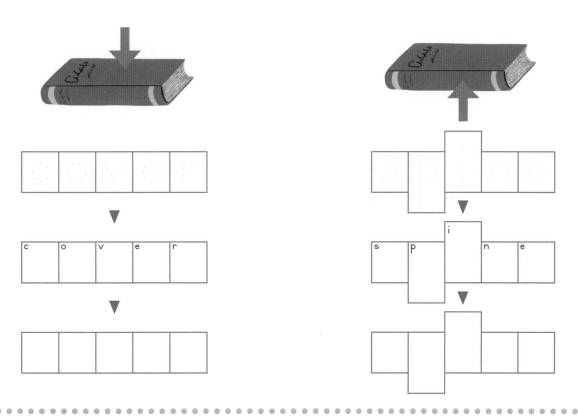

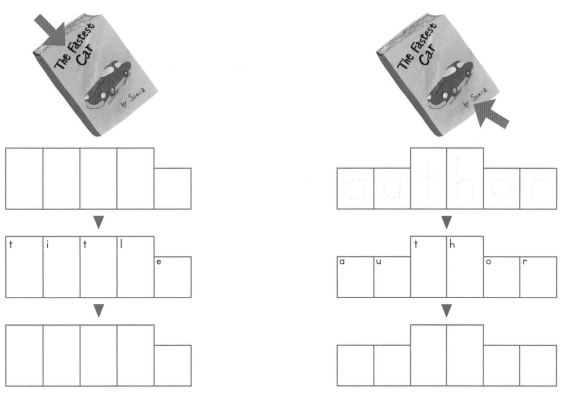

28 Language Arts Words
Words and Sentences

■ Trace the letters while saying each word.

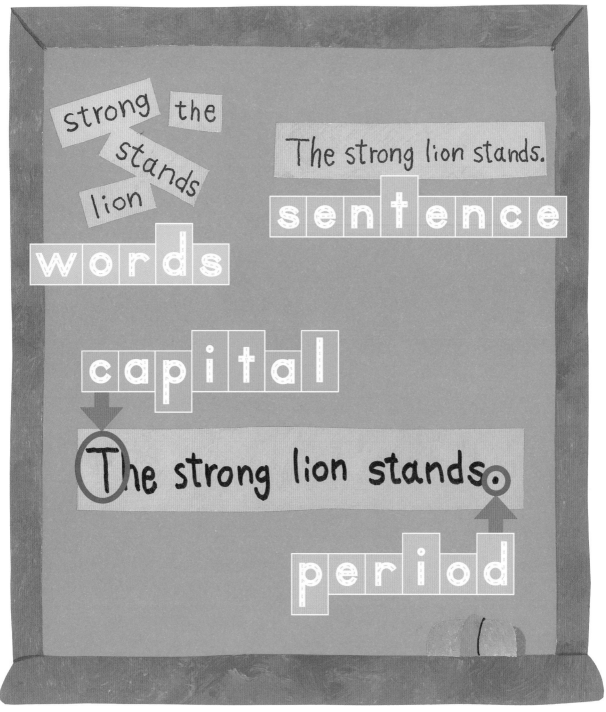

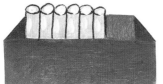

■ Trace the letters while saying each word.

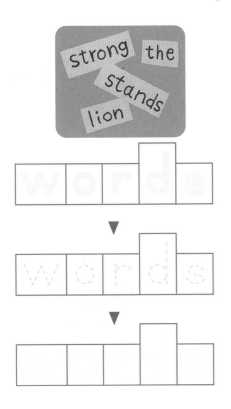

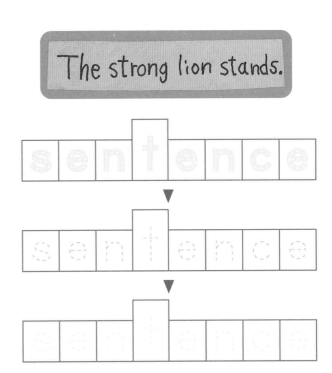

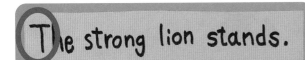

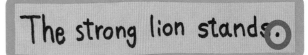

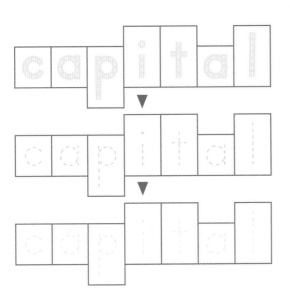

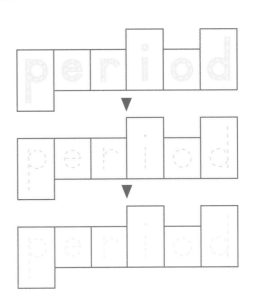

29

Language Arts Words
Words and Sentences

Name

Date

■ Trace each word. Then match each word with the correct picture.

words ●

★ The strong lion stands.

sentence ●

★ strong the stands lion

capital ●

★ The strong lion stands.

period ●

★ The strong lion stands.

■ Trace and write the letters while saying each word.

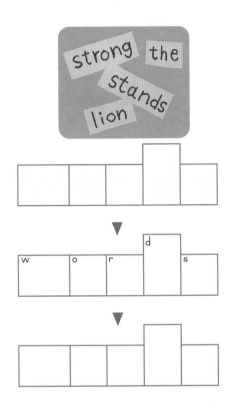

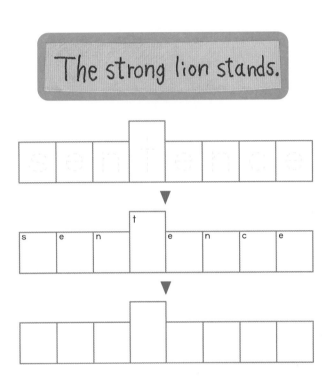

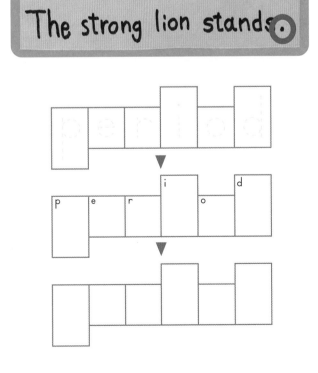

30

Language Arts Words
Review

■ Write the letters while saying each word.

c o v e r

w o r d s

strong the stands lion

s p i n e

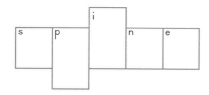

s e n t e n c e

The strong lion stands.

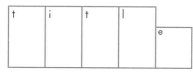

t i t l e

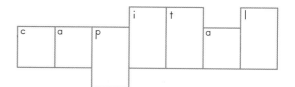

c a p i t a l

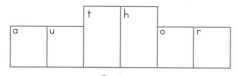

The strong lion stands.

a u t h o r

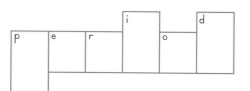

p e r i o d

The strong lion stands.

To parents/guardians:
This is the last page of this section before the final review. As an added challenge, the words on this page now appear in a mixed-up order. If your child has difficulty, help them focus on one word at a time.

■ Write the letters while saying each word.

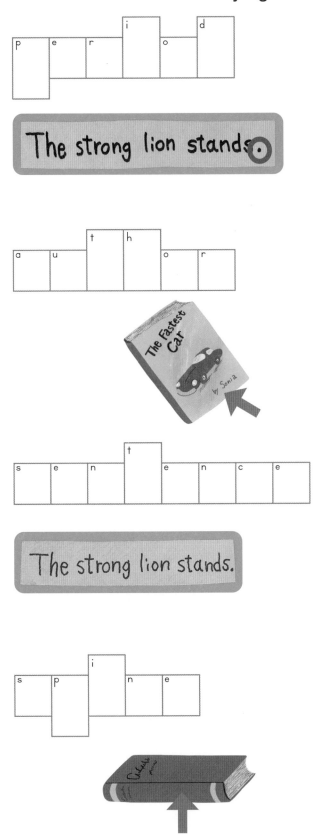

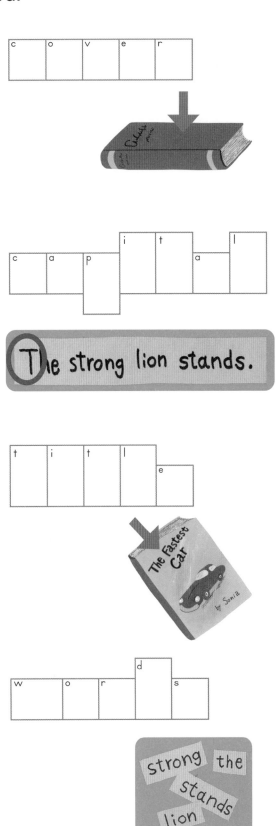

141

Review
Science Words

Name

Date

■ Write the letters while saying each word.

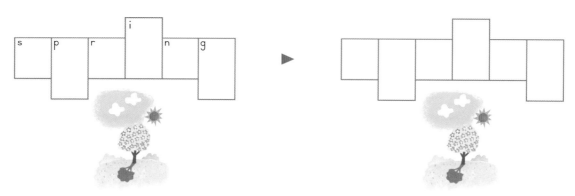

s p r i n g

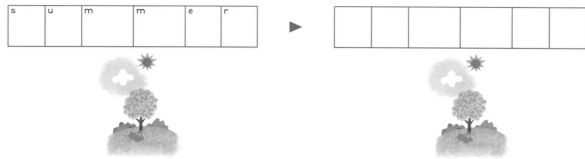

s u m m e r

f a l l

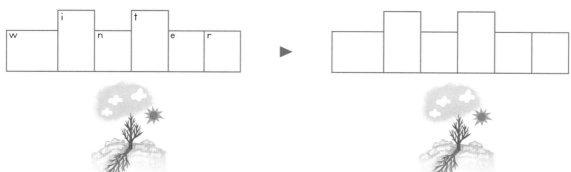

w i n t e r

142

■ Write the letters while saying each word.

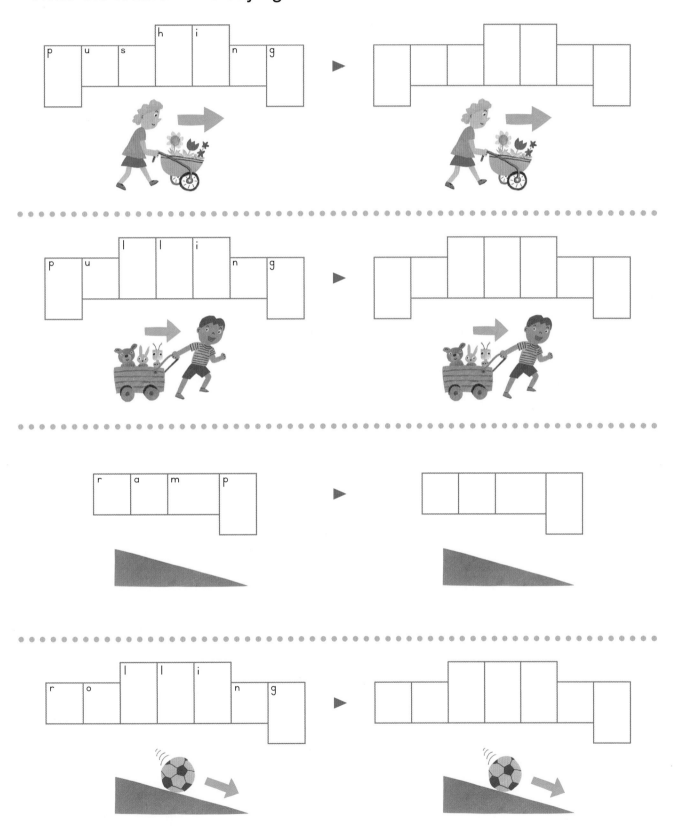

Name

Date

■ Write the letters while saying each word.

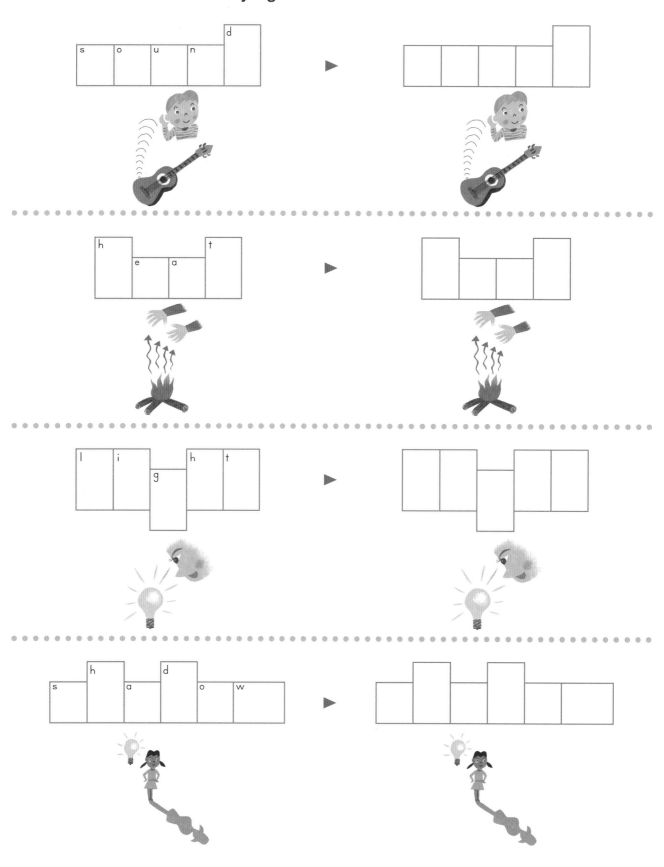

■ Write the letters while saying each word.

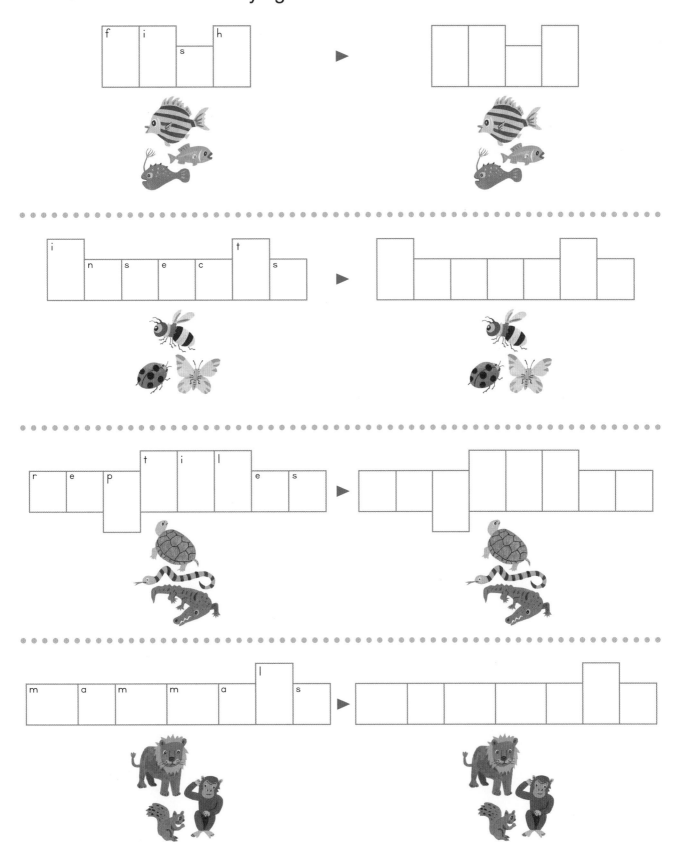

Name

Date

■ Write the letters while saying each word.

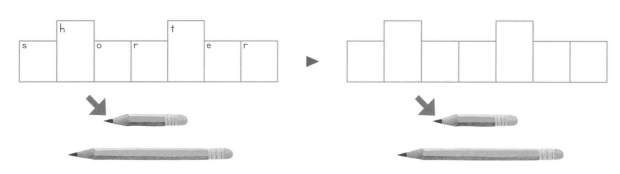

s h o r t e r

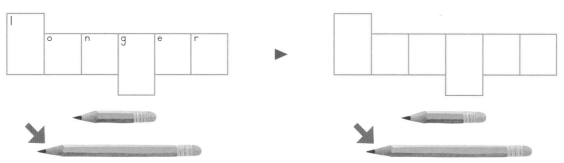

l o n g e r

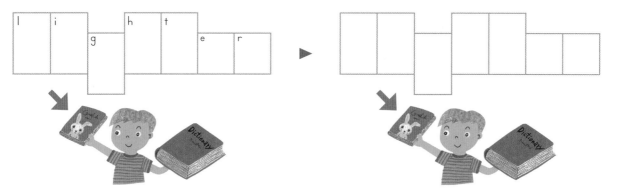

l i g h t e r

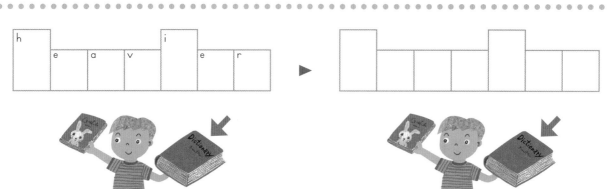

h e a v i e r

■ Write the letters while saying each word.

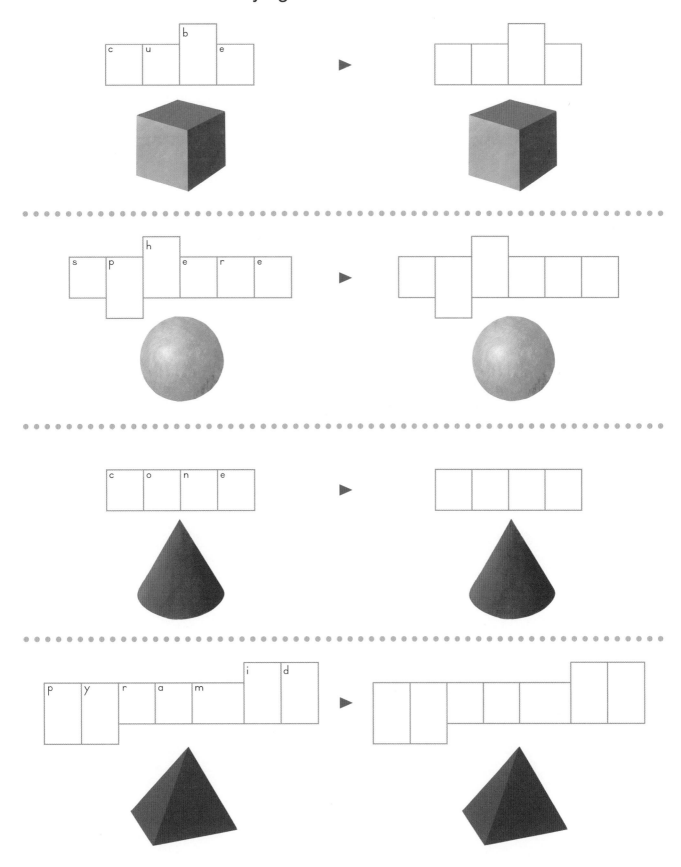

Review
Math Words

Name

Date

■ Write the letters while saying each word.

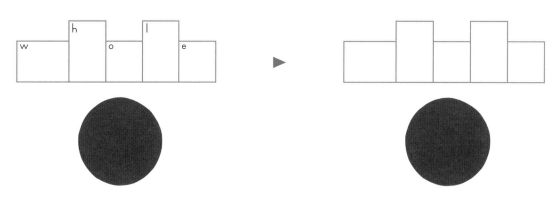

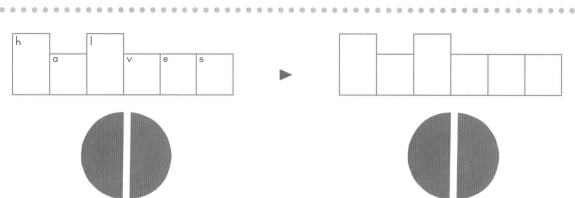

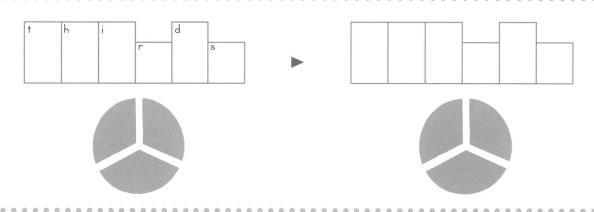

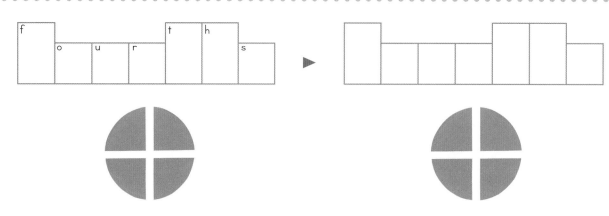

Review
Social Studies Words

Name

Date

■ Write the letters while saying each word.

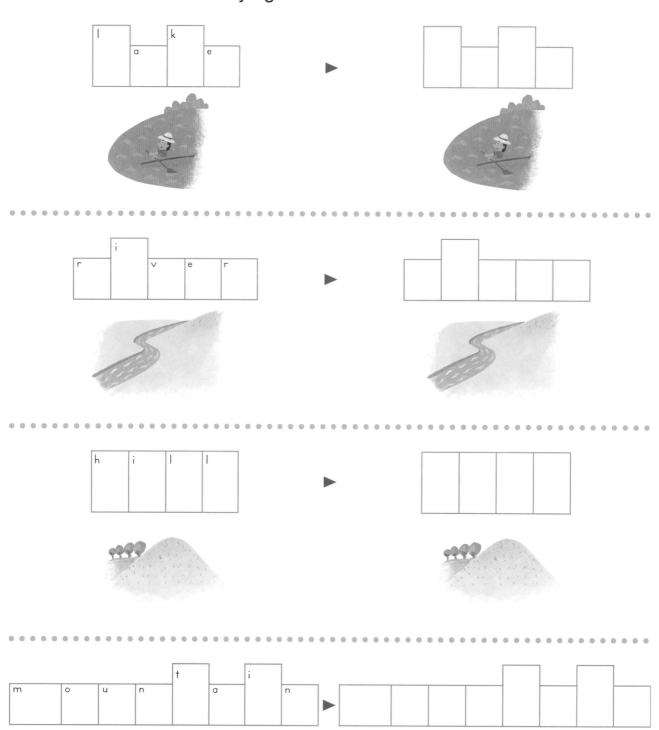

■ Write the letters while saying each word.

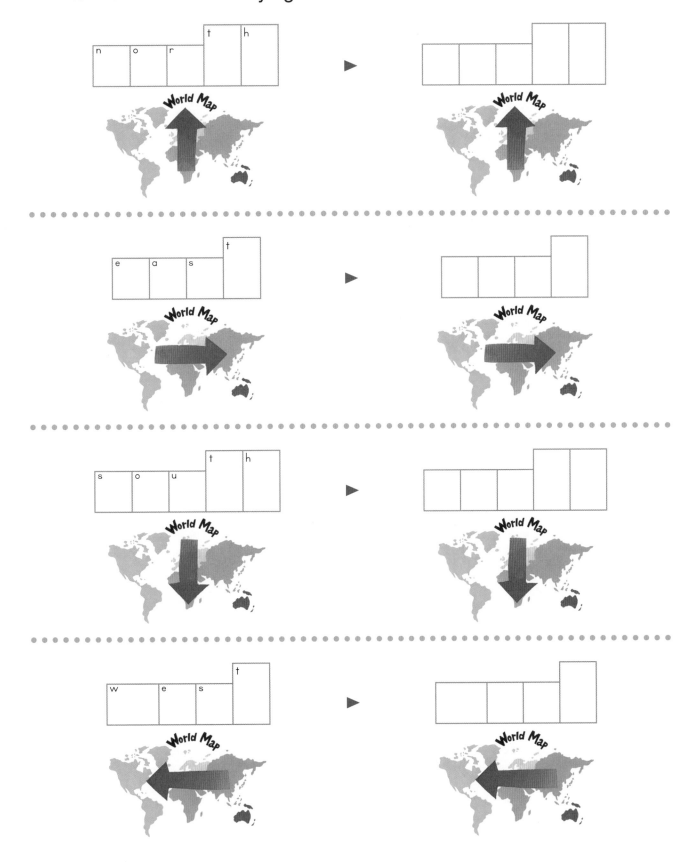

Name

Date

■ Write the letters while saying each word.

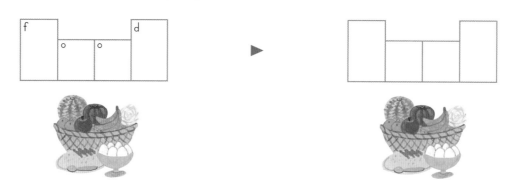

f o o d

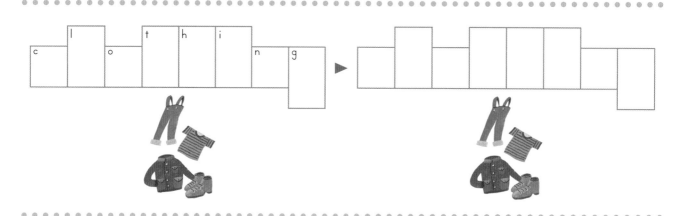

c l o t h i n g

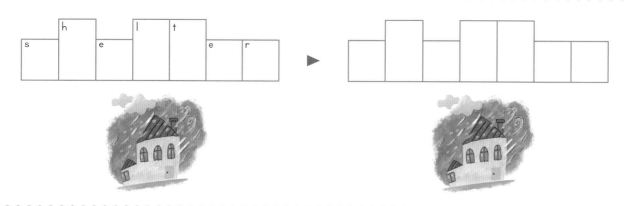

s h e l t e r

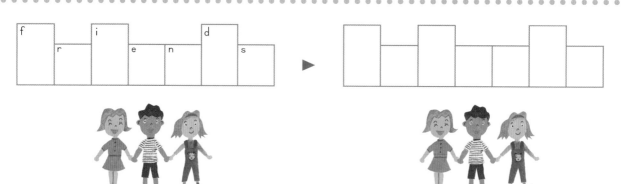

f r i e n d s

■ Write the letters while saying each word.

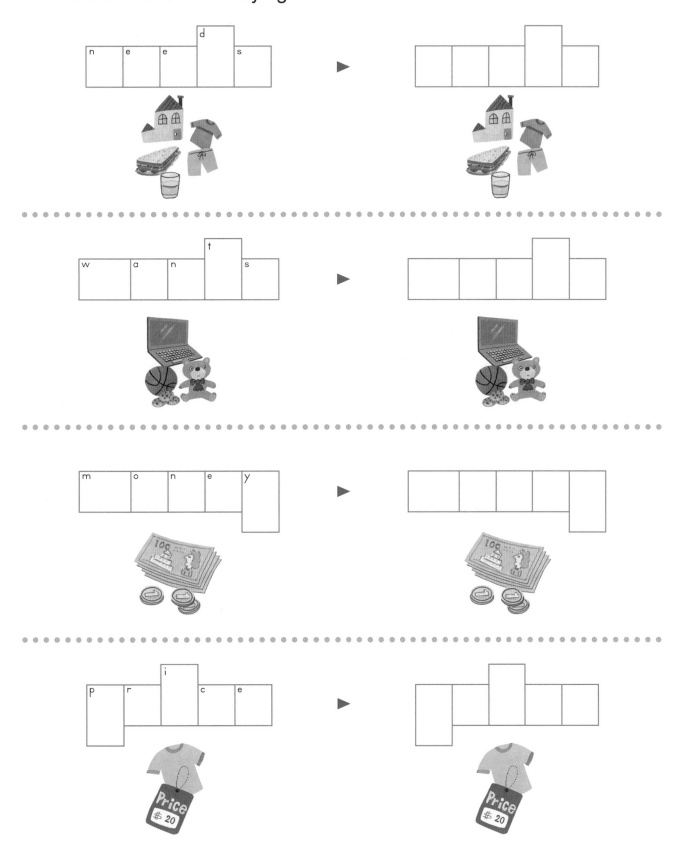

Name

Date

■ Write the letters while saying each word.

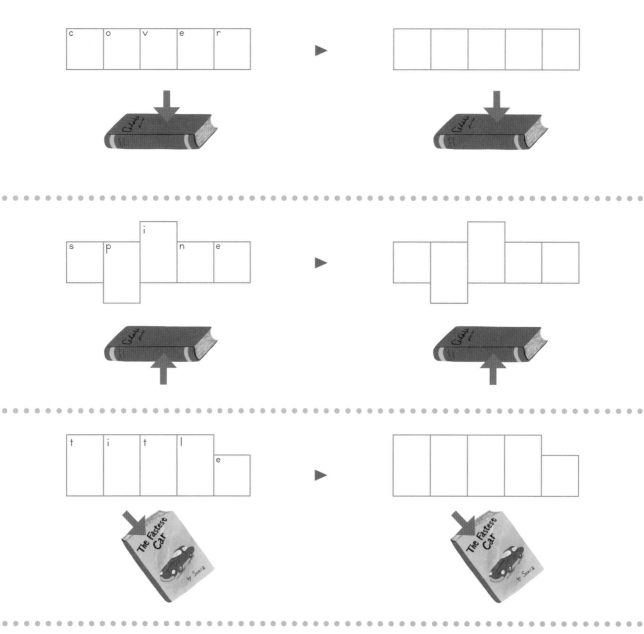

c o v e r

s p i n e

t i t l e

a u t h o r

To parents/guardians:
This is the last exercise of this workbook. Please praise
your child for the effort it took to complete this workbook.

■ Write the letters while saying each word.

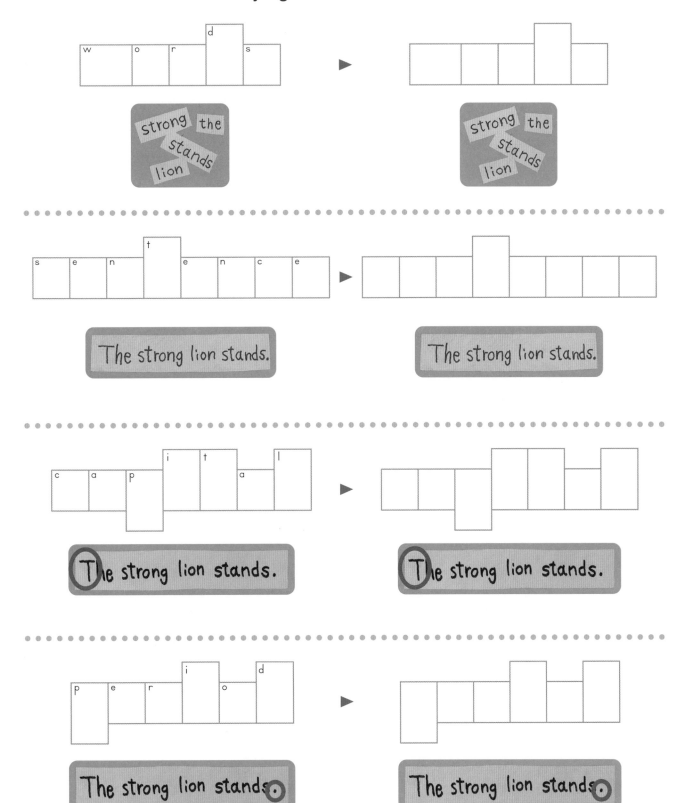

Answer Key

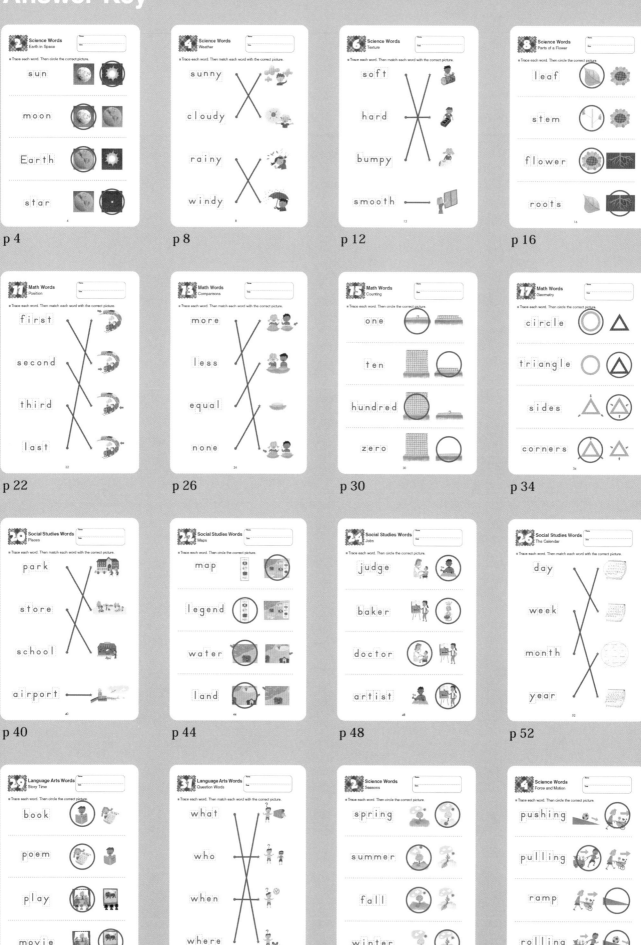

p 4

p 8

p 12

p 16

p 22

p 26

p 30

p 34

p 40

p 44

p 48

p 52

p 58

p 62

p 84

p 88

Answer Key

p 92

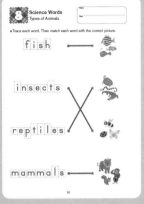

p 96

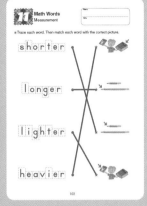

p 102

p 106

p 110

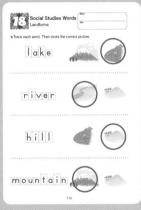

p 116

p 120

p 124

p 128

p 134

p 138

157

Answer Key

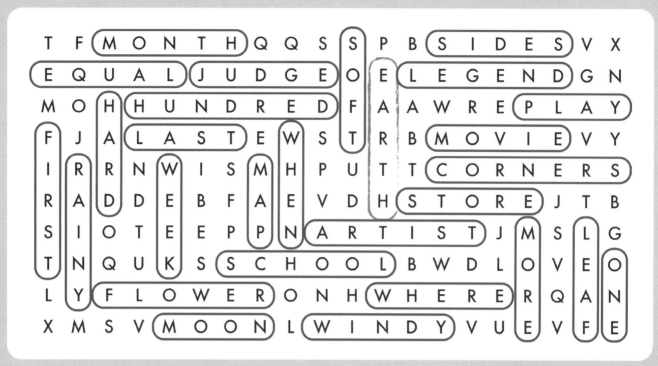

Word Search

Crossword Puzzle

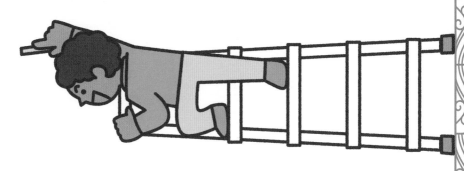

KUM◯N

Certificate of
Achievement

. . . .

is hereby congratulated on completing

My First **WORDS** for **SCHOOL**

Presented on . . . . , 20 . . . .

. . . .

Parent or Guardian